Disaster Risk Reduction and Management in India

Emerging Challenges and Way Forward

Disaster Risk Reduction and Management in India

Emerging Challenges and Way Forward

Editors

Sigamani Panneer

Santosh Kumar | Balu I

Vigneshwaran Subbiah Akkayasamy

B L O O M S B U R Y

NEW DELHI • LONDON • OXFORD • NEW YORK • SYDNEY

BLOOMSBURY INDIA
Bloomsbury Publishing India Pvt. Ltd
Second Floor, LSC Building No. 4, DDA Complex,
Pocket C – 6 & 7, Vasant Kunj,
New Delhi 110070

BLOOMSBURY, BLOOMSBURY PRIME and the Diana logo are trademarks of Bloomsbury Publishing Plc

First published in India 2022
This edition published 2022

ISBN: 978-93-54357-57-2
2 4 6 8 10 9 7 5 3 1

Typeset by Fortune Graphics, Naraina, New Delhi
Printed and bound in India by Replika Press Pvt. Ltd

Contents

Foreword

The word disaster has become familiar to every person. Communities are learning how to survive a disaster, overcome it, and readapt to any situation. The United Nations Office for Disaster Risk reduction reports that India has been affected by 321 incidences of natural disasters in the last two decades.India is anation with the third-largest number of disasters in the world with China and America being the first and second, respectively This data does not include manmade disasters still the intensity, frequency, and effect of these disasters remain very high.

A fragile ecosystem, extreme climate changes, and in some cases sheer negligence, has caused many of the greatest disasters. Jim Wallis, an American Theologist and Political activist rightly said, 'Sometimes it takes a natural disaster to reveal a Social Disaster'. In the cycle of disaster management and risk reduction, it has become essential to not only understand and assess the vulnerability based on geographical factors but also take into account social vulnerability. Socially disadvantaged communities are more vulnerable to disasters and their after-effects. This class nature of the disaster impact has been greatly experienced during the lockdown to combat COVID-19. The protected fear the loss of economic growth and social life whereas the unprotected fear the risk of hunger, loss of daily work, and physical wellbeing. The aim of training officials of health, education, rural development, women and child welfare, social welfare, local governance bodies, non-governmental organisations, law enforcement, and other welfare-related professionals and researchers is to help them understand the changing face of disaster management. It may be impossible to prevent the occurrence of a natural disaster, however with effective training, knowledge and expertise, it may be possible to help mitigate the effects and handle a disaster more efficiently.

The focus for this book is not only on traditional approaches to disaster but also to understand the need for a systematic approach to identify, assess,and reduce the risk of disaster. During this pandemic, lessons were learnt on how to survive. We also focus on the ways of building resilience in various sectors of health, agriculture, education, animal husbandry, revenue, transport, public works, water and electricity, law enforcement, rescue, and relief. The role of the public sector to invest in these areas must be risk-informed and sustainable to reduce human cost, economic losses, and ultimately be able to transform lives.

In the implementation of the disaster management measures, it is essential that the public sector as well as non-governmental sector, must be trained and prepared to address the more specific needs of vulnerable populations and ensure to bridge the gap between the 'protected' and the 'unprotected'. This efficiency can only be achieved when challenges and gaps can be identified and addressed. The current disaster management risk reduction frameworks lack qualified and trained human resources, national-level coordination, and follow inadequate understanding as well as a not so unified response framework. This requires public strategies to cope with not only disaster response but also disaster prevention and mitigation.

To conclude, it can be stated that the very act of recognising any harmful phenomena as a disaster or a formal declaration of it as one will emphasise its importance and thereby reduce the risk factors associated with it. As said, 'Knowledge is power', alayman's know-how on how to handle disaster alongside the public sector's assistance will be invaluable in dealing with risk management. For the future, we need to ensure that aspects such as disaster loss information, disaster effects on mental health, and its impact on society and the environment are complied and assessed, to judge the degree of the calamity thereby helping various stakeholders to be better prepared to respond and deal with further disasters.

I take this moment to congratulate the editors, authors, and co-authors who contributed papers for this book. My gratitude to the National Institute of Disaster Management, Ministry of Home Affairs, Government of India, New Delhi, Chief Patron and Patrons of the Programme of which this book is the outcome.

Prof. Dr M. Krishnan, M.Sc, PhD.
Vice-Chancellor,
Central University of Tamil Nadu,
Thiruvarur

Preface

Disasters tend to pose a threat to all elements of human life, including progress on the Human Development Index (HDI). When a calamity happens, it not only has a detrimental impact on a developing country's Gross domestic product, but also sets back plans by a significant length of time. Various disaster-prevention measures are undertaken by governments and private organisations to lower the risk in social, economic, and environmental terms. There are various barriers to disaster risk reduction, along with a lack of procedures for organising disaster risk assessment data, a lack of local-level capacity development, and challenges obtaining political and financial backing.

While disaster management efforts have been taken, there is still a long way to go in terms of enacting policies for disaster risk reduction in all aspects of life, as the 15th finance commission has for the first time set out certain priority areas and provided guidelines on how disaster funds can be used efficiently by forcing astate to invest on it.

Hence, it is necessary to bring together educational institutions, academicians, governments, and private stakeholders to explore how risk might be shared and managed. This book aims to shed light on the COVID-19 Pandemic crisis, flood physical vulnerability, mental health in disaster risk reduction, child inclusive disaster risk management, and other direct and indirect repercussions in the country's economic and development debate in this context. The book's chapters are multidisciplinary, with knowledge and ideas from several professions such as social work, economics, geography, and public policy expected to be shared.

Editors

Acknowledgements

I thankfully acknowledge the authors and co-authors who contributed chapters for the online training programme on 'Emerging Challenges for Disaster Risk Reduction: New Strategy and 15th Finance Commission'. On behalf of the editorial team, I convey my deep gratitude to Professor Dr M. Krishnan (M.Sc, PhD), Vice-Chancellor, Central University of Tamil Nadu, Thiruvarur; Shri Taj Hassan, IPS Executive Director (Additional Charge) National Institute of Disaster Management, Ministry of Home Affairs, Govt. of India, New Delhi; Professor Y. Satyanarayana, Founding Vice-chancellor, Damodaram Sanjivayya National Law University, and Former Vice-Chancellor, AP Law University, Visakhapatnam; and Professor Dr B. Ramaswamy, Honourable Vice-Chancellor, Om Parkash Jogender Singh University, Rajasthan for their immense support and encouragement towards this joint initiative. I convey my deep gratitude to Professor Santosh Kumar, Professor and Head, Governance and Inclusive Disaster Risk Reduction Division, National Institute of Disaster Management, Delhi and Balu I, Child Centric Disaster Risk Reduction Centre, National Institute of Disaster Management, Delhi for extensive academic collaboration.

Sigamani Panneer
Professorand Head,
School of Social Sciences and Humanities,
The Department of Social Work,
The Central University of Tamil Nadu,
Thiruvarur, India

Prologue

Disaster Management in India: Emerging Challenges

In the twenty-first century, natural disasters are becoming increasingly prevalent, stressing the importance of disaster risk reduction and management. Disasters can be catastrophic to communities and set back development efforts greatly. However, in the aftermath of a tragedy, it may provide an opportunity to invest in development activities. Communities rebuild themselves by identifying their strengths aftermath of the disaster. The current global scenario necessitates worldwide initiatives to manage the impact of natural disasters and advancements. With increasing floods to droughts, natural disasters continue to be a major issue for India which the country needs to handle efficiently and effectively.

The extent of vulnerabilities of various populations who experience significant losses of the disaster determines disaster risks. In several nations, the developmental approach has a substantial influence on disaster risk. Disaster recovery will become potentially catastrophic for poverty-stricken nations, thus it is vital to adopt disaster management systems that include mitigation, readiness, quick response, and faster recovery on the one hand, and development initiatives on the other. In the last two decades, the volume of natural activity has increased dramatically. When we glance at India's profile, we can see that no part of the country is immune to calamities such as droughts, strong rainfall, earthquakes, urban flooding, tsunamis, landslides, and so on.

Strategies for Disaster Risk Reduction in India

To address disasters and pandemic health situations in India, improved regional communication and coordination are required. The consequences of disaster can be combated by combining locally available resources, technology, and innovations such as risk analytics, telemedicine, tele-education, and distant learning. Preparedness with Disaster Risk Reduction techniques saves lives and protects individuals in crisis during a disaster. The Disaster Risk Reduction process includes earlier detection, early warning, fast diagnostics, risk management, communications, telehealth, and provision of services. Multi-stakeholder engagement, risk research and data, best practices, policy guidelines, resources, and building capacity can all help in the development of positive and productive intervention programmes to meet the requirements of all sectors of the community affected by disasters. Individuals, communities, districts, states, and the nation as a whole should all work together to reduce risk.

In this context, this book attempts to shed light on the Covid-19 Pandemic Crisis, Physical Vulnerability of Floods, Mental Health in Disaster Risk Reduction, Child Inclusive Disaster Risk Management, and other direct and indirect implications in the country's economic and development discourse. The Chapters in the book follow a multidisciplinary approach, that provide knowledge and ideas from a variety of fields, including social work, economics, geography, and public policy.

Objectives of the Book

The objectives of the book are to explain the impacts of disaster on development and to identify and list new emerging challenges in disaster risk reduction. The book also attempts to explain the process of mainstreaming disaster risk reduction into the development plan and to draft and apply strategies for the new emerging challenges in disaster risk reduction.

Scope of the Book

Whenever a disaster strikes, the most marginalized people are affected, including economically disadvantaged populations, children and women, the elderly and disabled, persons with chronic health problems, people living in isolated rural and urban regions with restricted access to healthcare care, and migrants. The scope of this book is so wide that it will serve as a foundation for understanding the risk and consequences of disasters, as well as their impact on the nation's development, forming a network of multi-sectoral agencies to develop comprehensive disaster management methods, and informing the public and policymakers about the role of multi-stakeholder engagement in disaster response. This book focuses on the importance of conducting in-depth research on disaster risk reduction.

Chapter Framework

Chapter 1 aims to study the vulnerability conditions of Chennai towards floods. As many cities are having riverine and coastal locations, floods are the most common urban disaster that leads to loss of life and property. Though the number of flood events increased worldwide the number of deaths has been decreased. Unprecedented urbanization, unplanned developments, land use land cover changes due to anthropogenic activities, and changing climate are the main causes of urban flooding. Being a megacity, Chennai is highly urbanized and often experiences the worst flooding situations.

Chapter 2 is based on the selected officially published articles and reports from various Journals, global and local governance bodies on their status of the Covid-19 Virus. The pandemic of Covid-19 has affected more than 181 countries making it difficult to predict its long term effects on humankind. The occurrence of the second wave of the pandemic is an open threat to society and human lives and it is a serious huddle for humankind in all the dimensional aspects of development. The government and the non-governmental agencies attempt their best possible output in controlling the impacts and damages made by Covid-19. The dimensions focused in this chapter include economic, business, ethical, social, environmental, territorial, and political, governance and public health.

Chapter 3 aims to highlight mental health problems, occupational health, challenges faced by the health care professionals during the Covid-19 pandemic. Health care workers are first-line warriors handling patients with Covid-19. They are exposed to a protracted source of discomfort which may exceed their coping skills. Maladaptive coping, a lack of training, and a lack of social support are among the major risk factors related to mental health disorders among health workers. The chapter also aims to suggest suitable interventions to address the mental health needs of the health care professionals in India. Besides, this might help the public health care system to recognize the causes of the mental health issues with health care workers and to provide effective intervention to face the health challenges posed by Covid-19.

Chapter 4 documents the evidence from the prevailing literature with an emphasis on Integrating Mental Health care in Disaster Risk Reduction, its rationale and necessity. In recent decades, Disasters have become a common occurrence in human lives. Understanding the Disaster Risk Reduction mechanism and strategies, learning how to strengthen them periodically is the only modality envisaged now. It is necessary to examine and disseminate the data predominant in this field, understand the strengths and inadequacies of the existing literature in both local and global contexts and improvise the developing knowledge in this regard accordingly. This chapter also tries to find ways to deal with it to thwart more such calamities and loss of human lives and resources.

Chapter 5 aims to analyze the awareness of child-centric disaster risk reduction among the stakeholders in India. A multi-stage sampling method was used in this study. This study was conducted in Kerala, Odisha, Maharashtra, Punjab and Tripura covering 300 respondents. The study found that only one-fourth of stakeholders are having good and poor awareness respectively. Awareness of CCDRR in the country is not satisfactory. Female stakeholders are having better awareness than male stakeholders. Civil society organization has good awareness than government officers. Stakeholders from the women & child welfare and revenue department are having better awareness than other departments. It is found that there is a strong association between states, departments and awareness.

Chapter 6 is about the wage loss of the construction workers of Tirupattur in Tamil Nadu. Primary data were collected from 150 construction workers based on random sampling during the pandemic period. The collected data was analyzed with the help of logistic regression analysis to identify the factors influencing wage loss of construction workers during the Covid-19 pandemic. The results of the study indicate the positive relationship between wage loss and Covid-19 pandemic.

Chapter 7 examines the Covid-19 and its impact on the Tamil Nadu economy from a macro perspective during the period of the first lockdown of March 31, 2020, to 3rd May 2020. There are extensive studies that explored how covid-19 affected in Indian economy However, there are limited studies to explore the regional perspective. In this context, this study examines the Covid-19 and its impact on the Tamil Nadu economy. This chapter is based on secondary data and the data obtained from sources of Statistical Hand Book of Tamil Nadu, Tamil Nadu Economic Appraisal and Centre for Monitoring Indian Economy.

Chapter 8 attempts to explain the retrieval of the food service industry (FSI) after the impact of Covid-19, with special reference to Coimbatore. The FSI was one of the hardest hit during the outbreak of covid 19 as they were shut down to control the spread of the virus across society. Covid 19 pandemic almost nullified the organized and unorganized restaurant business across the country. Measures (Lockdown, social distancing, dine in restrictions) adopted by the government to slow down the spread of the virus, imparted huge loss to the FSI that severely affected the livelihood of millions of restaurant workers in the country with Coimbatore as no exception. The findings of the chapter may identify the factors that need to be tapped and frame a strategy to increase sales to increase the sales volume. Moreover, it provides a significant contribution to the literature to find out the effects of the pandemic as well as other crises on the FSI.

Chapter 9 represents the keynote presentations of the eminent speakers invited from the UK, Japan, Australia, Germany, South Africa, Afghanistan and India for an International Virtual Symposium titled, 'Pandemics, Climate Change and Growing Inequality: Emerging Paradigm Shift in Helping Professions', the chapter explores Social pandemics, Covid-19 lockdown effects and responses, Crisis preparedness and management, Community based actions as the influential factors that determine the emerging paradigms in Social Work and Public health. The socio-economic and cultural determinants of health and health systems across the globe are challenged swiftly by the Covid-19 pandemic, witnessing a humanitarian crisis in many parts of the world. In this chapter, Technological innovation, climate change adversities and the scope of the helping professions are also briefed. The chapter identifies thrust areas for the future direction of research, professional practice and shares key learning and recommendations.

Chapter 10 presents various discussions and deliberations that took place in the three-day workshop organized by the Central University of Tamil Nadu in collaboration with the National Institute of Disaster Management on "Emerging challenges for disaster risk reduction: New strategy and 15th finance commission". Natural disasters have become more common in recent years, emphasizing the need for disaster risk management and disaster risk reduction. The development process has a significant impact on disaster risk, in most countries; the development process has a significant impact on disaster risk. The training sessions stressed the importance of Multi-stakeholders' participation, Risk data and information, good practice, policy guidance, tools and capacity building can support in designing constructive intervention programmes to address the needs of all sections of the community affected by the disaster.

Sigamani Panneer, Santhosh Kumar,
Balu I. and Vigneshwaran Subbiah Akkayasamy

CHAPTER 1

Assessment of Physical Vulnerability to Floods: A Case Study of Chennai City, India

SULOCHANA SHEKHAR[1] AND SARATH. R[2]

Abstract: *As many cities have riverine and coastal locations, floods are the most common urban disaster that leads to the loss of life and property. Though the number of flood events increased worldwide, the number of deaths has been decreased due to disaster preparedness and mitigation measures. Unprecedented urbanization, unplanned developments, land use, land cover changes due to anthropogenic activities, and changing climate are the leading causes of urban flooding. Being a megacity, Chennai is highly urbanized and often experiences the worst flooding situations. Therefore, this study focuses on the vulnerability conditions of Chennai towards floods. Reducing the risk associated with urban floods needs proper planning with effective preparedness and mitigation measures. For that, one should understand the vulnerable areas of the city region, and there are various methods available for assessing multiple kinds of vulnerability. Physical vulnerability is the most critical one, and analyzing the physical vulnerability is the need of the hour. Though different approaches are available for assessing the physical vulnerability, an indicator-based method has been used in this study with selected parameters based on the literature, time, and cost. Built-up density, elevation, distance from water bodies, shoreline, flood exposed areas, building roof and walls, and population density, are the parameters used in the weighted overlay analysis carried out in this study to understand the physical vulnerability. The final results showed that 20.3 per cent of Chennai city is highly vulnerable to floods, and 79 per cent is moderately vulnerable. That seeks the attention of city planners, administrators, and all other stakeholders to work together and plan effectively to reduce the risk of floods.*

---

[1] Professor and Head, The Department of Geography, Central University of Tamil Nadu, Thiruvarur, India

[2] Research Scholar, The Department of Geography, Central University of Tamil Nadu, Thiruvarur, India

Keywords: Urban Flood, Physical Vulnerability, Chennai, Weighted Overlay, GIS

Introduction

The extent and occurrence of floods and their effect on elements at risk have increased worldwide and are probably the number one cause of losses (Quevauviller, 2014; Jha et al., 2012; Kron W, 2005). Though mortalities from significant disasters have decreased, the number of incidents causing deaths, to a minimum of a hundred, and property damage has been rising steadily (Burtan et al., 1993). The Asian region in particular experiences flood disasters of high magnitude very often, and shows the same pattern of a decrease in the number of deaths but a notable increase in the number of people affected, and also an increase in the economic losses (ADPC, 2007; Ciurean et al., 2013).

As many cities have riverine and coastal locations, floods are the most common urban disaster that leads to the loss of life and property (Zevenbergen et al., 2010). The city administrations have the crucial responsibility of managing floods protecting people and their environment, particularly when they have a riverine or coastal location. The urban local bodies need to enhance disaster resilience and reduce vulnerability through proper planning and actual implementation. The first step in this process is to measure and map the spatial vulnerability (Takemoto, 2011). The vulnerability analysis includes analyzing physical, social, and economic factors.

Physical vulnerability describes the built environment's ability to withstand impacts, including all types of buildings, roads, bridges, etc. According to Van and Kingma (2011), 'physical vulnerability refers to the potential for physical impact on the built environment and the population.' They stated that:

> "It can be relatively quantified as it is directly dependent on the physical impact of a hazard event, and it relates to the magnitude and intensity of the hazard, and the characteristics of the elements at risk."

The physical vulnerability may be determined by population density level, settlement distance from water bodies, size, design, and build-up materials used for basic infrastructure and housing (UNISDR, 2004). When a flood occurs, most of the damages caused are physical factors and pose a significant threat. A weak structure of a building may fall on people during a flood and increase the risk; poorly developed soils may uproot trees and add further danger. So, a proper understanding of vulnerable regions must be made to appropriate mitigation strategies and lessen the damages and losses. There is a need for an integrated flood management system (Büchele et al., 2006).

Geographic Information System (GIS) based urban flood zoning was done using the parameters such as distance to water bodies, terrain conditions, groundwater table depths, and urban land use/land cover to quantify the vulnerability (Fernandez et al., 2010; Ozkan and Tarhan, 2016; Chen et al., 2009; Wang et al., 2018). A similar assessment has been followed in this study using elevation parameters, distance from shoreline and water bodies, built-up area density, and the percentage of concrete roofs and concrete walls. The population density parameter is also chosen as a critical factor that adds vulnerability to disasters.

To understand the physical vulnerability towards flood, the Chennai city region has been chosen, which is highly urbanized and is a low-lying area towards the eastern coast of India. Chennai experiences frequent floods. Though causes are artificial, most of the damages are caused by physical factors, posing a significant threat. This chapter attempts to classify the city based on its physical vulnerability using geospatial tools and techniques (Kourgialas and Karatzas, 2011; Lee et al., 2018; Miguel et al., 2021). The work focuses on assessing the critical parameters of urban flooding using weighted overlay multicriteria evaluation to identify various categories of flood vulnerability zones (Kubal et al., 2009).

Study Area

Chennai is the capital city of Tamil Nadu State. According to the 2011 Indian census, India's sixth-most populous city and fourth-most populated urban agglomeration. It is a megacity with high intensity of urban sprawl (Devi et al., 2019). Chennai, often referred to as the 'Gateway to South India,' is located on the south-eastern coast of India. In the north-eastern part of Tamil Nadu on a flat coastal plain known as the Coromandel coast (Map 1). Its average elevation is around 6.7 meters, and its highest point is 60 meters (District Profile, 2017).

Chennai is located in a tropical region with a mean annual temperature of 24.3°C to 32.9°C. Late May to early June is the hottest part of the year with maximum temperatures peaking between 35°C and 40°C, while January with minimum temperatures around 15°C to 22°C is considered the coolest part of the year. The humidity usually ranges between 65 per

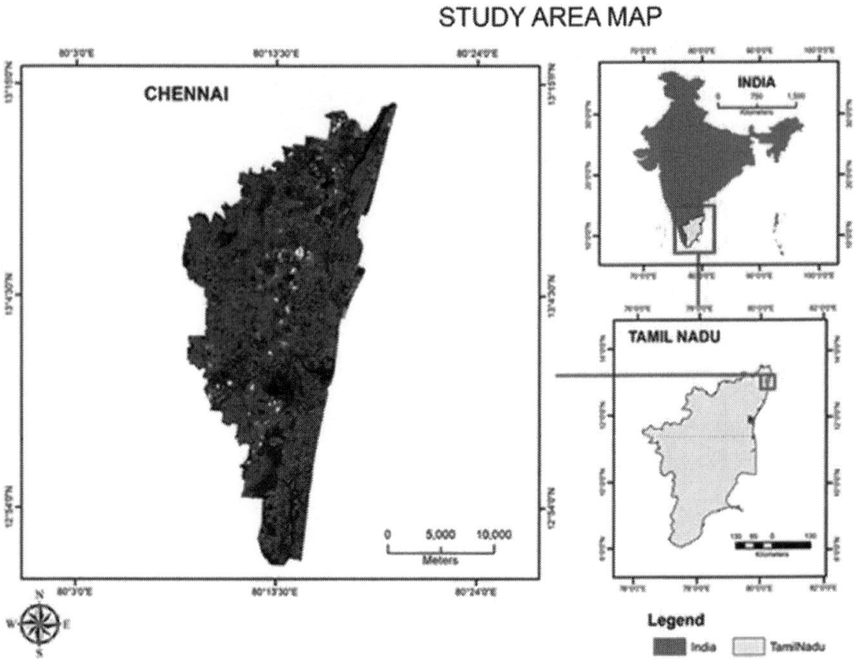

Map 1: Location of Chennai

cent and 84 per cent. Chennai usually experiences southwesterly winds between April and October and northeasterly winds during the rest of the year. The northeast monsoon brings the rains during October, November, and December with an average annual rainfall of 1200 millimeters (CMDA, 2008).

Cooum and Adyar are the two major rivers that flow through the center and south of Chennai. These rivers are linked by the Buckingham Canal that runs parallel to the coast. The Otteri Nullah (Nullah refers to a small stream) runs in the east-west direction and meets the canal at Basin Bridge. Kortalaiyar, the third river, flows through the northern fringes of Chennai. Other than these significant water bodies, several lakes of varying sizes are located on the city's western boundaries and serve as a natural habitat for numerous species of birds and animals (District Profile, 2017).

Materials

This study heavily depends on secondary data. Sentinel 2B imagery of 10-meter spatial resolution acquired on 1 January 2021 was used for built-up area mapping, extracting drainages, and shoreline. The data was used to obtain the base map for Chennai through digitization along with the coastline and water bodies.

Shuttle Radar Topography Mission Digital Elevation Model (SRTM DEM) was used to obtain the elevation values of the study area. Elevation plays a significant role in assessing vulnerability as low-lying areas are more prone to flooding. The SRTM DEM has a resolution of 30 meters.

The Census 2011 data was used for obtaining the population data, which was further used to calculate the population density. Data regarding the roofing material and wall material were also obtained from Census 2011. The District Handbook of Chennai, Kancheepuram, and Thiruvallur was used to obtain the population of 200 wards in Chennai. The Greater Chennai Corporation Disaster Management Plan, 2017, was used to get the regions affected by floods during 2015 in Chennai.

Methodology

There are various methods adopted in measuring physical vulnerability, and among them, the indicator-based methodologies are well known for assessing vulnerability (Figure 1). This method provides a broader, speedy, and reliable evaluation of flood vulnerability in a specific geographical region (Nasiri et al., 2016).

Indicator-based method, curve method, disaster loss data, and models approach are diverse techniques for evaluating flood risk and vulnerability.

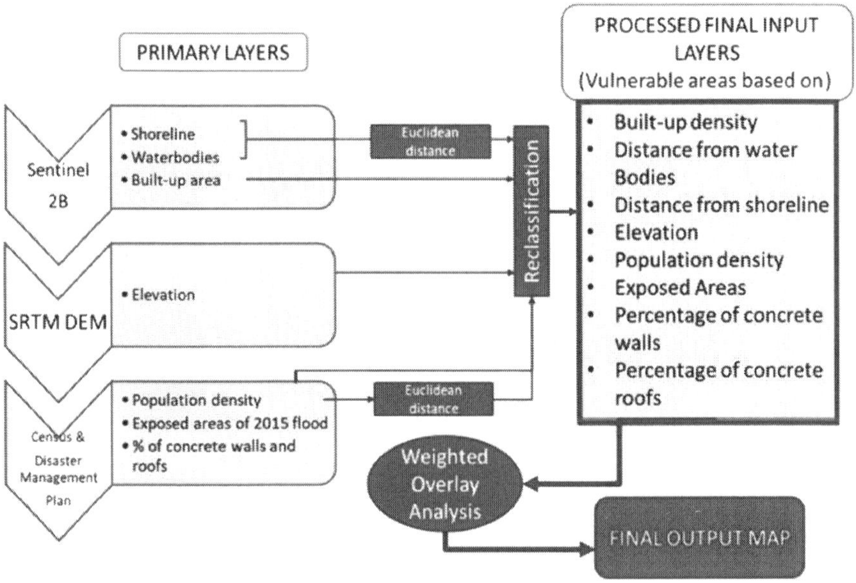

Figure 1: Methodology

The indicator approach is tricky because the accessibility of good data and the number of the indicators are very hard to quantify, especially social indicators (Nasiri et al., 2016). In the present work, due to the covid pandemic, primary data collection was highly restricted. Therefore, the study was based on satellite data-derived indicators: built-up density, distance from water bodies, shoreline, and flood exposed areas. Other indicators such as population density and building materials were taken from Census 2011 data published by the Office of the Registrar General and Census Commissioner, India (ORGI).

The built-up area and water bodies were extracted using the maximum likelihood classification tool from sentinel imagery. The output rasters were then converted to shapefile format using the raster to polygon tool. The built-up area (Map 2a) was selected and exported from the classification output as a built-up layer. The intersection was carried out with the Chennai Corporation ward layer. Then using the field calculator, the built-up density for each ward was calculated using the formula,

$$\text{Built-up density (\%)} = \frac{\text{Built-up area of the ward}}{\text{Total area of the ward}} \times 100$$

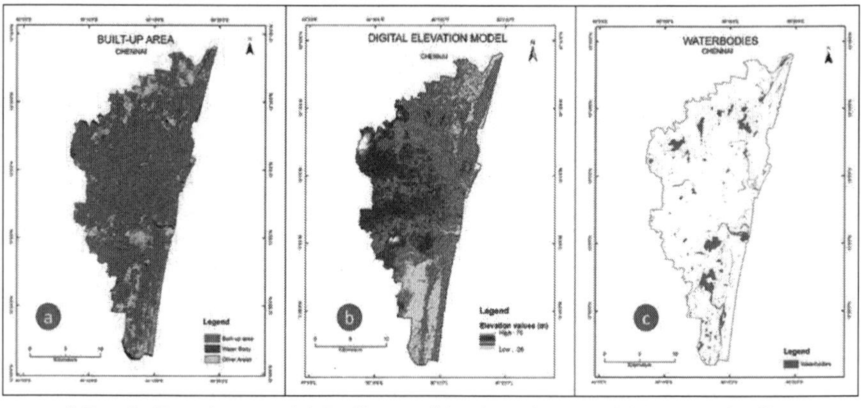

Map 2: Baselayers: (a) Built-up, (b) Elevation, and (c) Waterbodies

Shuttle Radar Topography Mission Digital Elevation Model (SRTM DEM) was acquired for the study area, and using the reclassify tool, the elevation raster (Map 2b) was obtained. The shoreline layer (Map 3b) was also extracted from the sentinel image, and the buffer zones around them were calculated by the Euclidean distance tool in ArcGIS. The population distribution map layer (Map 3a) was created using the data from the district handbook for Chennai, Thiruvallur, and Kancheepuram districts. The areas that were inundated during the 2015 flood were identified from the disaster management plan published in 2017 and from newspaper articles through the internet to create the inundation layer. The percentage density of wall material was calculated from the District Handbook of Chennai, Thiruvallur, and Kancheepuram districts (Map 4).

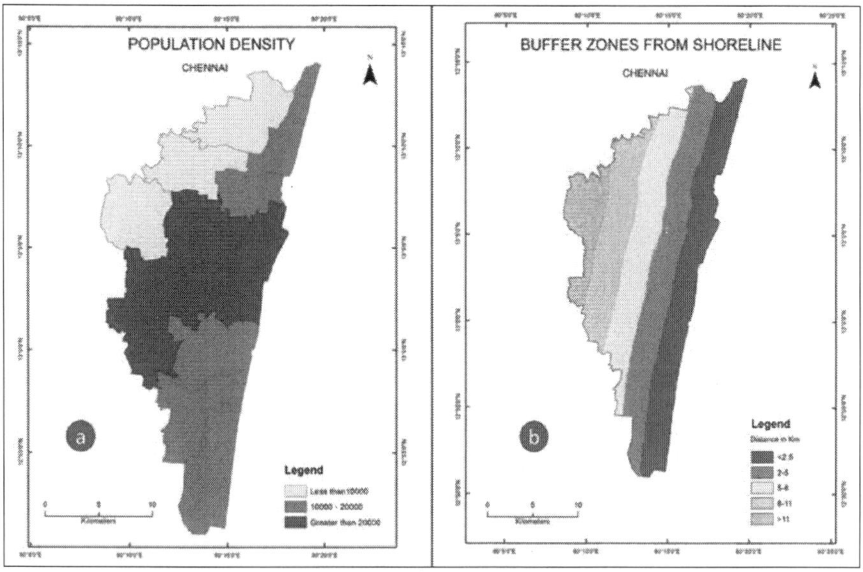

Map 3: Baselayers: (a) Population Density, and (b) Shoreline Buffers

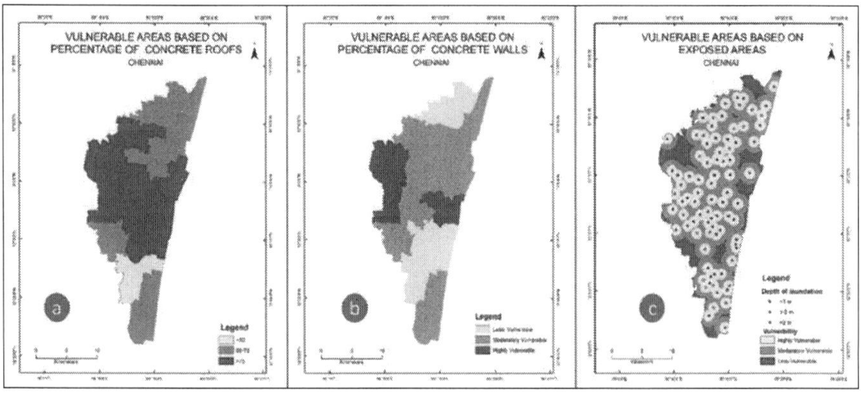

Map 4: Baselayers: (a) Concrete Roofs, (b) Walls, and (c) Exposed Areas to Flood

The flood exposed areas were taken from the Disaster Management Plan of Chennai. The areas were identified on Google Earth images as point locations and exported as .kml files. Then, they were converted to .csv files, and point data was obtained from them through ArcGIS. The buffers were then created around them using Euclidean distance (Map 4).

Once the base layers were ready, they were reclassified into three classes as less vulnerable, moderately vulnerable, and highly vulnerable areas to flooding based in Table 1, and scores were assigned. The high vulnerability zone received the highest score. The layers were then used for weighted overlay analysis by giving weightage to each layer

Table 1: Scoring Criteria Used for Reclassification of the Considered Factors that Affect Physical Vulnerability

Factors	*Classes*	*Score*	*Vulnerability Level*
Built-up density (%)	<50	1	Low
	50–75	2	Moderate
	>75	3	High
Proximity to Waterbodies (km)	<1	3	High
	1–2	2	Moderate
	>2	1	Low
Proximity to Shoreline (km)	<3	3	High
	3–8	2	Moderate
	>8	1	Low
Proximity to exposed areas (km)	<1	3	High
	1-2	2	Moderate
	>2	1	Low
Elevation (m)	<5	3	High
	5–15	2	Moderate
	>15	1	Low
Population density	<10,000	1	Low
	10,000–20,000	2	Moderate
	>20,000	3	High
Ward-wise concrete roofs (%)	<50	3	High
	50–75	2	Moderate
	>75	1	Low
Ward-wise concrete walls (%)	<15	3	High
	15–20	2	Moderate
	>20	1	Low

Table 2: Weightage Given for Layers Used for Overlay Analysis

Layer	*Weightage*	*Layer*	*Weightage*
Population density	10	Distance from shoreline	10
Exposed areas	10	Built-up density	15
Elevation	15	Percentage of concrete roof	15
Drainage	10	Percentage of concrete wall	15

as mentioned in Table 2, and the study area was classified into high, moderate, and low physical vulnerable regions.

The reclassification of base layers and weights assigned to all parameters were based on available literature and as discussed in the Disaster Management Plan of Chennai (2017).

Results and Discussion

Once the base layers were prepared, the maps were then reclassified to get an integer raster needed for the vulnerability assessment. The built-up layer was reclassified into three classes based on the built-up density, with more than 75 per cent as highly vulnerable, between 50 per cent and 75 per cent as moderately vulnerable, and less than 50 per cent as less vulnerable. The water bodies layer was reclassified into three classes where the highly vulnerable area is 1 kilometer from water bodies, 1–2 kilometers is moderately vulnerable, and above 2 kilometers is less vulnerable. The scoring was generally done based on the available literature. The shoreline reclassification was done such that less than 3 kilometers from the shore are highly vulnerable, and greater than 8 kilometers are less vulnerable. The moderately vulnerable areas lie between them (Map 5).

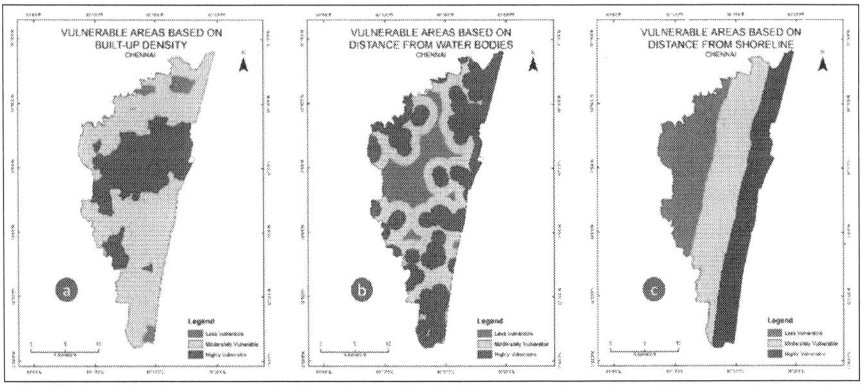

Map 5: Vulnerability Maps: (a) Built-up, (b) Water bodies, and (c) Shoreline

The elevation raster was reclassified into less than 5 meters, 5–15 meters, greater than 15 meters, the lowest being the most vulnerable. The population map was reclassified based on population density greater than 20,000 as highly vulnerable and less than 10,000 as less vulnerable. The exposed areas to flood were then reclassified as highly vulnerable zones falling under 1 kilometer from the point buffer and less vulnerable areas greater than 2 kilometers (Map 6).

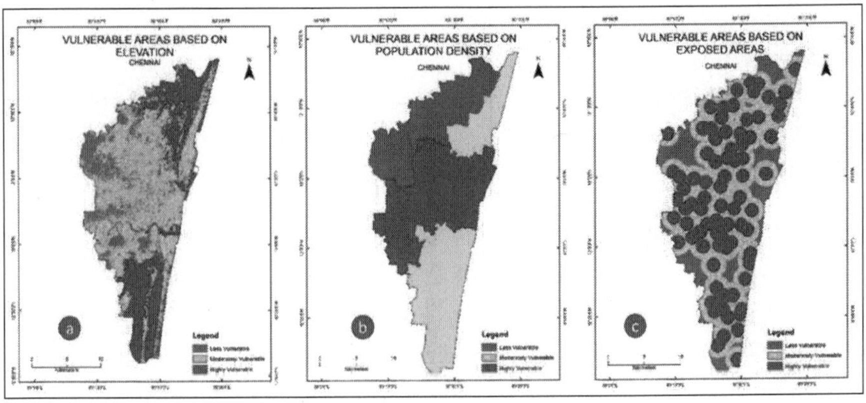

Map 6: Vulnerability Maps: (a) Elevation, (b) Population Density, and (c) Exposed Areas to Flood

Similarly, for the wall materials, the zones with a percentage density of less than 15 per cent of concrete walls were classified as highly vulnerable, and those with a higher percentage density above 20 per cent were classified as least vulnerable. Similarly, the percentage density of concrete roofs was obtained. Those zones with values less than 50 per cent were classified as highly vulnerable, and those above 75 per cent were least vulnerable (Map 7).

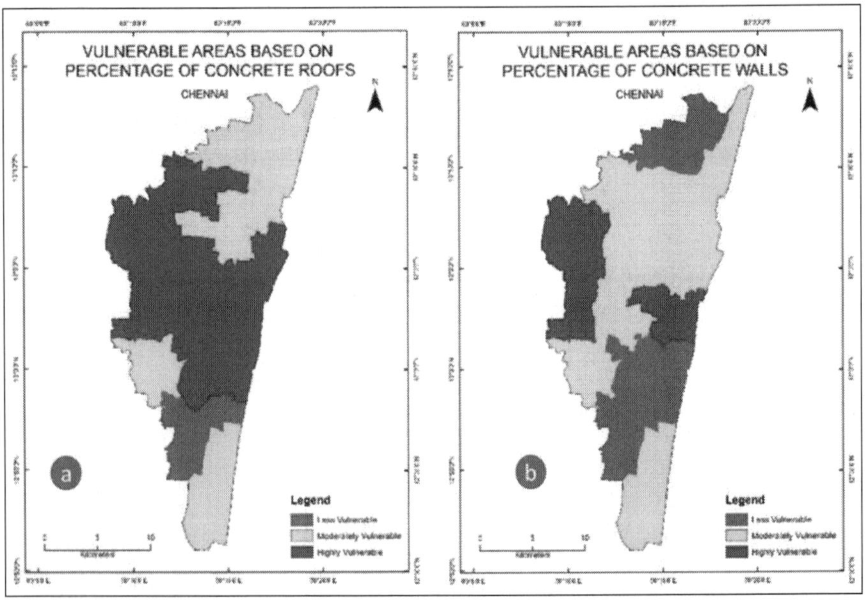

Map 7: Vulnerability Maps: (a) Concrete Roofs, and (b) Wall Materials

The weighted overlay analysis was done in ArcGIS as per the weightage given in Table 2 for physical vulnerability assessment by overlaying all parameters (previously inundated areas, built-up density, elevation, distance from water bodies and shoreline, percentage of concrete roofs, percentage of concrete walls, and population density). The compiled weighted overlay output was obtained, which illustrates the vulnerable areas on the scale of three levels, namely low, moderate, and high. The final result of this study (Map 8) indicates that 20.3 per cent of the study area is highly vulnerable, and 79 per cent is moderately vulnerable. Only less than 1 per cent of Chennai is exposed to less physical vulnerability. Rapid urbanization, unplanned development, and changing climatic conditions are the major causes (Price, R. K., and Vojinovic, Z, 2008) for urban floods in Chennai (Lavanya and A. K., 2012).

If all the parameters are individually analyzed, the results showed that the study area is exposed to high vulnerability because of water bodies and high population density. A moderate level of exposure is observed for more than 50 per cent in most cases. Earlier studies proved that structural types made of a wood wall, wood floor, and galvanized iron sheet roof are most vulnerable to floods, while the least vulnerable is the structural

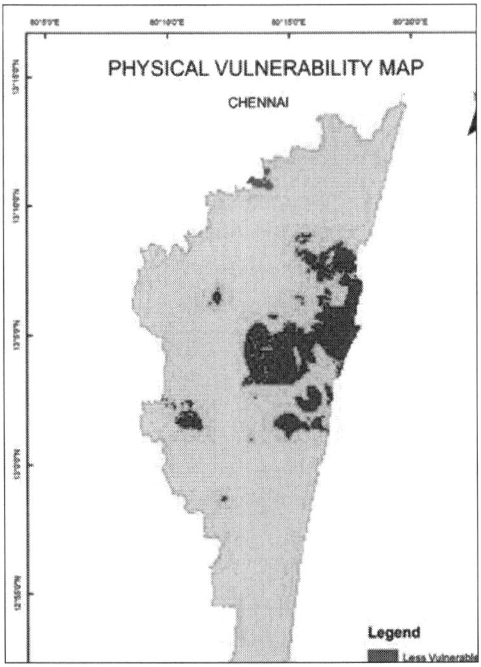

Map 8: Final Output Map Showing Physically Vulnerable Areas of Chennai

type made of a concrete wall, ceramic tiles floor, and steel sheet roof (Chinyere. A, 2005). The lack of concrete ceilings and walls exposed the study area to moderate physical vulnerability.

The vulnerability map showed that most of the study area is moderately vulnerable to physical factors that cause a flood. The study area is a highly urbanized region in South India, and it is a megacity with more than 10 million population. The high degree of urbanization led to converting open land, wetland, dry channels, lakes, and other green spaces into built-up land. The increased built-up land reduced infiltration, enhanced surface runoff, and made the city vulnerable to floods (Jamali B. et al., 2018). Even though no field data is used and decade-old census data is taken for this study, it proves that a significant portion of the city is moderately vulnerable to floods and needs proper disaster risk management. So, more parameters like building types, number of floors, materials used to construct, depth of floodwater, and other social parameters are needed to assess its vulnerability to the actual reality. The developmental activities that took place cannot be reversed. The only possible way to overcome the vulnerable situation is to properly manage existing properties and ensure that future developmental activities must be strictly monitored. Sustainable urban development measures should be promoted in urban areas. Necessary mitigation and disaster preparedness plans should be taken during the pre-monsoon period, and the stormwater drainage system needs to be strengthened.

Limitations

The present work was based only on open-source satellite data products and Census data. No primary survey was possible due to covid lockdown. Because of this, the key parameters such as floodwater depth level in the exposed areas, number of floors in a building, building age, and quality of construction materials were not included in the study. There was no financial support to get the high-resolution data products.

Conclusion

Chennai city is highly urbanized and is still expanding, due to which, the natural ecological balance is highly disturbed. The rivers deviate from their natural flow path, shrunken drainages, reduced infiltration capacity due to increased built-up, and plain terrain make the city more vulnerable. The analysis concluded that elevation, built-up, population, proximity to seashore and water bodies are essential and fundamental indicators of physical vulnerability to flooding. The method of weighted overlay analysis concluded that Chennai is mainly exposed to moderate physical vulnerability to flooding, i.e. urban flood in specific. The physical vulnerability assessment done in this study gives an idea of the spatial distribution of the vulnerable areas that will help in the mitigation process and in adopting planning strategies.

References

[1] ADPC (2007). 'The Primer on Integrated Flood Risk Management in Asia', Asian Disaster Preparedness Center.

[2] B. Büchele, H. Kreibich, A. Kron, A. Thieken, J. Ihringer, P. Oberle, F. Nestmann (2006). 'Flood risk mapping: Contributions towards an enhanced assessment of extreme events and associated risks'. *Natural Hazards and Earth System Sciences*, 6, 483–503.

[3] I. Burton et al. (1993). 'The Environment as Hazard', 2nd edition, Guilford Press.

[4] Census (2011). Population Tables, Office of the Registrar General and Census Commissioner, India (ORGI).

[5] J. Chen, A. Hill, A., and L. D. Urbano (2009). 'A GIS-based model for urban flood inundation'. *Journal of Hydrology*, 373(1-2), 184–192.

[6] A. Chinyere (2015). 'Assessment of physical vulnerability to flood in Saint Lucia'. *Case Studies: Castries old Central Business District and Dennery Village M.S. Thesis*, University of Twente, Enschede.

[7] R. Ciurean., D. Schröter., and T. Glade (2013). 'Conceptual Frameworks of Vulnerability Assessments for Natural Disasters Reduction'. *Approaches to Disaster Management – Examining the Implications of Hazards, Emergencies and Disasters*, 3–32. doi:10.5772/55538

[8] CMDA (2008). '2nd Master Plan for Chennai Metropolitan Area – 2026'. http://www.cmdachennai.gov.in/Volume1_English_PDF/Vol1_Chapter00_Introduction.pdf

[9] N.N. Devi., B. Sridharan, and S.N. Kuiry (2019). 'Impact of urban sprawl on future flooding in Chennai city, India'. *Journal of Hydrology*, 574, 486-496.

[10] District Profile (2017). Chennai district.

[11] D.S. Fernandez, and M.A. Lutz (2010). 'Urban flood hazard zoning in Tucumán Province, Argentina, using GIS and multicriteria decision analysis'. *Engineering Geology*, 111(1-4), 90-98.

[12] B. Jamali, R. Löwe, P.M. Bach, C. Urich, K. Arnbjerg-Nielsen, and A. Deletic (2018). 'A rapid urban flood inundation and damage assessment model'. *Journal of Hydrology*, 564, 1085–1098.

[13] A.K. Jha, R. Bloch, and J. Lamond (2012). 'Cities and Flooding'. *A Guide to Integrated Urban Flood Risk Management for the 21st Century.* Washington, DC: World Bank. doi:10.1596/978-0-8213-8866-2

[14] N.N. Kourgialas, and G.P. Karatzas (2011). 'Flood management and a GIS modelling method to assess flood-hazard areas – A case study'. *Hydrological Sciences Journal – Journal des Sciences Hydrologiques*, 56(2), 212–225.

[15] W. Kron (2005). Flood risk = hazard • values • vulnerability. *Water international*, 30(1), 58–68.

[16] C. Kubal, D. Haase, V. Meyer, and S. Scheuer (2009). 'Integrated urban flood risk assessment – Adapting a multicriteria approach to a city'. *Natural hazards and earth system sciences*, 9(6), 1881–1895.

[17] A.K. Lavanya (2012). 'Urban flood management – A case study of Chennai city'. *Architecture Research*, 2(6), 115–121.

[18] S. Lee, S. Lee, M.J. Lee, and H.S. Jung (2018). 'Spatial assessment of urban flood susceptibility using data mining and Geographic Information System (GIS) tools'. *Sustainability*, 10(3), 648.

[19] Miguel Leal, Eusébio Reis, Susana Pereira, and Pedro Pinto Santos (2021). 'Physical vulnerability assessment to flash floods using an indicator-based methodology based on building properties and flow parameters'. *Journal of Flood Risk Management*, Volume 14, Issue 3, September 2021. e12712.

[20] Nasiri, Hajar and Mohd Yusof, Mohd Johari and Ali, Thamer (2016). 'An overview to flood vulnerability assessment methods'. *Sustainable Water Resources Management*, 2. 10.1007/s40899-016-0051-x.

[21] S.P. Ozkan, and C. Tarhan (2016). 'Detection of flood hazard in urban areas using GIS: Izmir case'. *Procedia Technology*, 22, 373–381.

[22] R.K. Price, and Z. Vojinovic (2008). 'Urban flood disaster management'. *Urban Water Journal*, 5(3), 259–276.

[23] P. Quevauviller (2014). 'Hydrometeorological hazards: Interfacing science and policy', Chichester, John Wiley & Sons, 2014.

[24] S. Takemoto (2011). 'Moving towards climate smarts flood management in Bangkok and Tokyo – Master thesis'. Massachusetts Institute of technology.

[25] UN-ISDR (2004). 'Living with risk'. *A global review of disaster reduction initiatives* (Vol. 1). Geneva. doi:10.1016/0143-6228(95)90037-3

[26] C. Van Westen, and N. Kingma (2011). 'Session 5: A vulnerability assessment'. In Multi-hazard risk assessment. *Distance education course Guide book*. Twente: United Nations University-ITC School on Disaster GeoInformation Management (UNU-ITC DGIM).

[27] Y. Wang, A. Chen, S., G. Fu, S. Djordjević, C. Zhang, and D.A. Savić (2018). 'An integrated framework for high-resolution urban flood modelling considering multiple information sources and urban features'. *Environmental modelling & software*, 107, 85–95.

[28] Z. Chris, A.Cashman, N. Evelpidou, E. Pasche, S. Garvin, and Richard Ashley (2010). 'Urban flood management'. CRC Press, 2010.

Web Resources Used

[1] UNDRR, Definition and classification of Hazard, retrieved from https://www.undrr.org/publication/hazard-definition-and-classification-review, accessed on 20.04.2021.

[2] NRDC, What is urban flooding, retrieved from https://www.nrdc.org/experts/anna-weber/what-urban-flooding, accessed on 20.04.2021.

[3] GCC Disaster Management Plan 2017, retrieved from https://www.chennaicorporation.gov.in/onlinebooking/images/CDMPpercent20Bookpercent20Wrapperpercent20Fullpercent20Bookpercent20(percent20English).pdf.

CHAPTER 2

Second Wave of COVID-19 Pandemic: Global Governance Dimensions of the Crisis

RENALDO S RAJKUMAR[1] AND
F.X. LOVELINA LITTLE FLOWER[2]

Abstract: *COVID-19 was declared as a global pandemic by the World Health Organisation on March 11, 2020 creating an unrest and fear within the whole world. Though the humanity has come across experiencing and defeating many infectious agents in the past, pandemic caused by COVID-19 has gone beyond all the rest. The United Nations has called it the greatest test for the humankind to survive. It is a global battle which has already taken thousands of lives, putting a threat not only on the dimension of health but is also a multidimensional beast threatening economics, politics, society, human rights and every aspect of life. COVID-19 has affected more than 181 countries making it difficult to predict its long-term effects over the humankind. The re-emergence and re-infection of the virus which can be also termed as the second wave should be handled with due care and precaution. The occurrence of a second wave of the pandemic is an open threat to the society and human lives and it is a serious hurdle for the humankind in all the dimensional aspects of development. The government and the non-governmental agencies are attempting their best possible output in controlling the impacts and damages caused by COVID-19. Global and local governance are trying to ensure a stability in the system and have invested their knowledge and skills in drafting policy to ensure better living standards for all people during the crisis. Implementation of the schemes and policies strategically by the global nations are of utmost importance to overcome this global crisis as early as possible. The most critical aspects of overcoming adversity are unity, openness, and international cooperation. This review paper is based on the selected officially published articles and reports from various journals and global*

[1] PhD Scholar, The Department of Social Work, Bharathiar University, Coimbatore, India

[2] Professor and Head, The Department of Social Work, Bharathiar University, Coimbatore. E-mail: lovelinabu@gmail.com

and local governance bodies on their status of the COVID-19 virus. The dimensions focused in this review article include economical, business, ethical, social, environmental, territorial, political, governance, and public health.

Keywords: Pandemic, COVID-19 Virus, Governance, Crisis, Precautions, Policies

Introduction

A global disease outburst is called a pandemic (OSHA, 2009). Medical advancements in the last century towards communicable diseases have been effective. Some diseases still exist within few geographical locations while others have the capacity to multiply creating a situation of an epidemic or pandemic (EPRS, 2020 and ICM, 2017). Flu pandemic is the emergence of a new virus which spreads rapidly causing illness and fatality among people and living creatures globally (CDC, 2017). COVID-19 was declared as a global pandemic by the World Health Organisation (WHO) on March 11, 2020 (CIDRAP, 2020) creating an unrest and fear within mankind. Though the humanity has come across experiencing and defeating many infectious agents in the past, pandemic caused by COVID-19 has taken a huge toll over the current globalisation.

From the early 1700s, eight global pandemics have occurred globally and have been officially recorded and declared by international organizations (CIDRAP, 2020). The humankind has learnt its lessons from the previous impacts regarding pandemic on a multidimensional point of view. In the 1990s, the world has seen a positive connectivity through the concept of globalisation, witnessing the growth of humankind, poverty reduction, and innovations (World Economic Forum, 2020). Seventy five years after the world war, the world is once again preparing itself for a global battle called COVID-19 which has already taken hundreds and thousands of lives, posing a threat not only as health crisis rather as a multidimensional beast threatening economics, humanity, society, human rights and so on (UN, 2020). COVID-19 has affected more than 181 countries (Shrestha et al., 2020) making it difficult to predict its long term effects over mankind (Donthu et al., 2020).

The occurrence of second wave of the pandemic is an open threat to the society and human lives. It is a serious hurdle for humankind in all the aspects of development (Cacciapagilia et al., 2020). The government and the non-governmental agencies are implementing their best possible solutions to control the impacts and damages towards humankind due to COVID-19. Global and local governance are trying to ensure a stability in the system and have invested their knowledge and skills in drafting policy to ensure better living standards for all people during the crisis (Penninyton et al., 2020). Strategical implementation of schemes by the global nations has been found to be productive to overcome this global crisis as early as possible.

Background and Methods

The background and methodology adapted in this article 'Second Wave of COVID-19 Pandemic – Global Governance Dimension of the Crisis' is a collection of officially published articles and reports from various journals and global and local governance bodies on their status of the COVID-19 virus. The dimensions focused in this review article include economical, business, ethical, social, environmental, territorial, political, governance, and public health. The primary and secondary sources of data were examined from the official reports of government and non-governmental agencies and publications from peer reviewed journals. The reports from the United Nations (UN), International Labour Organisation (ILO), Sustainable Development Report, Organization for Economic Co-operation and Development (OECD), World Health Organisation (WHO), United Nation Development Programmes (UNDP), etc., were a valuable source of official and trustable information used in this study. Some published articles from reputed peer reviewed journals like Elsevier, Wiley, Taylor & Francis, SAGE, Springer, etc., were also used in this study that helped to visualise ideologies and information on a global researcher's point of view. To further add authenticity to the paper, few online published journals were also included. A total of 37 references of reports and journals have been widely incorporated in this study which includes 19 published journals and 18 reports from international and national agencies on COVID-19. Multiple checks on the information and data were carried out wherever it was possible.

Review Protocols

The fear of a pandemic has a long devastating history in the world. As we are trapped in the middle of a pandemic wave, it is difficult for us to calculate approximately the long term effects of COVID-19 especially on the following:

Economic and Business Factors

The outbreak has forced many economic shutdowns leading to disruption in global trade and business processes. Challenges like shortfall in workforce, cash flow, purchaser demand, marketing, sales, employment, trade, etc., determine a question of guarantee and promising future for the people involved and economy. The freedom of movement between humans has moved towards restrictions leading to limitations in job market and human workforce (Jose Alves et al., 2020). The consumers have also learnt to restrict themselves with their needs and wants. Internet and social media have restricted the interaction among people and profession as a whole. Some businesses are falling and some new adaptable businesses for the situation are emerging typically with innovations and inventions. The COVID-19 pandemic has made the world to be more conservative and protective in preserving the resources, keeping in mind the global challenges on economy and business (Donthu et al., 2020 and ILO, 2020).

A crisis being an unintended outcome, it is a threat to the ethical dimension of humankind. The effects of COVID-19 have had extraordinary impacts on global nations compared to previous pandemics like Severe Acute Respiratory Syndrome (SARS), H1N1, and Spanish Influenza. The first wave of this crisis constructed a threat to almost all the nations, leading to closure of borders. The livelihoods of the disadvantaged sects of people were put to a risk and their survival was an ethical question on the world nations. Crisis management on COVID-19 calculates the overall impact in terms of finance, legal, human, etc., but safety of the marginalised, vulnerable, and disadvantaged groups was failed to be covered on a whole which projects ethical instability and reflects discrimination in social and moral understanding of inclusive sustainable development (Sustainable Development Report, 2020 and Muller et al., 2020). An extreme crisis like COVID-19 has multiple perceptions towards global societies regarding social norms and individual behaviour with due responsibility. The global nations can combine together for a formation towards establishing an ethical web of relationships worldwide (Branicki, 2020).

Socio-economic Implications

The COVID-19 pandemic has reduced the efficiency of the global workforce across all the sectors of economy. Agriculture being a primary sector for majority of the global nations, its prices have dropped by 20 per cent on all commodities leading to labour scarcity thus, deteriorating the livelihood of farmers. The secondary sector, due to lack in export and import and inconsistent supply chain of raw materials, exhibited delay in production activities. Work from home concept, which was not applicable to the manufacturing sectors as compared to the information and communication sectors, has led to a deficiency in the reduction of global production and stock market. Tertiary sector institutions like the service sectors have seen a rapid fall due to the closure of borders, preventing visitors and tourists. Moreover, a decline in global stock market was an economic shock (EPRS, 2020). The fear of recession and socio-economic collapse occurring worldwide needs to be addressed through immediate relief measures for generating stability on the global and socio-economic development (Nicola et al., 2020 and Ito, 2020).

Environmental Impact

The environmental impact due to COVID-19 includes two areas to be focused during the global lockdown: (1) on the immediate effects on environment, and (2) long term changes in the environment. The pandemic has led to a positive approach towards a sustainable future with increase in resilience in socio-ecological system in a shorter span of time. The pandemic has caused the nations to have a concern for the environment, triggering improvement of ecological regain by controlling the consumption of waste and explosion of pollution which is harmful to the environment (CCSA, 2020). An organic lifestyle is flourishing once again, maintaining the natural ecosystem and the quality of air has improved as the emission of greenhouse gases has been controlled to some extent. Many world institutions working for environment have witnessed an improvement in resources like water, soil, ecology, climate change, etc. The emergence of this pandemic has re-established the unbreakable humanitarian bond with the nature (Cheval et al., 2020).

Territorial, Political and Governance

The COVID-19 pandemic, on a peculiar aspect, has its dimensional influence even towards the territorial, political and governance as these concepts may be slippery but can be constructed, and contested at any moment of time. The pandemic has made many countries to shut down their territorial borders and have restricted the invasion of non-residents and foreign citizens. The health control exchange measures, due to the pandemic, across the nations have stopped. The national and international transportation during emergency crisis was globally restricted. The pandemic have also put forth additional responsibility on the officials of national territories in which their power has rendered the vulnerable sections even weaker (UNCTAD, 2020).

Having a perspective for the global and national politics, national agencies and international bodies have articulated their strategy plans to reduce the communal spread of the virus. Opposition parties of many nations have criticised the ruling government estimating their outfall in prevention and policy implementation regarding the virus. Many global countries, through networking, have adapted the best practices in controlling the virus. On another perspective, there prevails an opportunity for the rising of a superpower in the global politics (UN, 2020).

Governance and administration is the backbone of any successful nation in terms of multidimensional development. The allocation of resources, monitoring and implementing the policies, engaging government and private sectors, and compromising with the population are some of the key activities of administration. The power play from the governance has also negatively affected livelihoods. Though this model has many different opinions on the positive and negative aspects, it needs to be accepted as such at one point because going forward experiencing challenges without a plan is always dangerous and risking the life of global population will outburst in revolution (Bernes et al., 2020 and Dodds et al., 2020).

Public Health

Public health during COVID-19 requires strategic moves under certain laws and policies like maintaining social distancing for preventing communal spread of the virus. International Health Regulations, 2005 has several obligations regarding public health emergency, national health surveillance, and disease related events. COVID-19 is a combat of biological, chemical, and radio nuclear hazard where the International Health Regulations, 2005 tends to develop disease surveillance, preparedness, capacity building, and mitigation of the risk (Nomani et al., 2020).

The concept of public health has a wide linkage with the sustainable development goals drafted in 2015 as majority of the seventeen goals listed in the United Nations focus on the health concept, directly or indirectly, giving more priority towards health. Many recent outbreaks on public health like H1N1, SARS, Middle East Respiratory Syndrome

(MERS), and EBOLA viruses, etc., had brought attention on neglected tropical diseases and inculcation of its severity helps to strengthen the health care systems of various nations (Heymann et al., 2020 and David M. et al., 2020). World Health Organisation along with many international bodies is continuously reviewing the assessments and progression in preventing communicable and non-communicable diseases which can become a threat to the public health. The recommendation for the future investments of the nations should be prioritised even for the public health as this pandemic is considered to be an intensive lesson on the importance of public health systems (ICM, 2017).

First Wave Analysis and Complexities

The COVID-19 virus has its first emergence in the Wuhan Province of China in December, 2019. The virus had a rapid spread across the globe as experienced public health experts of various nations failed to predict its severity on its initial evaluation (CIDRAP, 2020). The World Health Organisation from the initial stage of COVID-19 has monitored the intensity of the damage the virus has had on humans and the organisation also coordinates with the global nations facilitating exchange of knowledge and resources to overcome this virus (CCSA, 2020). By the month of June (2020), as recorded by WHO, the virus has infected 10 million people and has caused fatality of 500,000 people worldwide (UNCTAD, 2020) and more than half of the global population experienced lockdown leading to a fall of global economy between 6 per cent to 7.6 per cent (OECD, 2020). This intense recording of impacts it is considered to be a life threatening beast for humankind.

The United Nations Organisation has developed a three-point response system for managing the initial stage of pandemic: (1) comprehensive health response, (2) safeguard life and livelihood, and (3) through recovery build back a better inclusive society (UN, 2020). The shortage in global health care services and an increase in demand for wide range of health care professionals like nurses, physicians, pharmacists, technicians, administrators, social workers, housekeeping, and mortuary personnel need to be trained in order to cope with the required demands (OSHA, 2009). The first wave has brought a complex situation not only in the global health care system but also in the economic, political, social, and environmental dimensions and they have also influenced both positive and negative aspects. Demand for food and water, handling natural disasters, financial and business crisis was an unacceptable controversy for many of the global government (ICM, 2017).

COVID-19 affects not only those who are infected but also puts others at risk. An infection cannot be controlled if people cannot afford testing or treatment. Governments have struggled in the past in controlling various epidemics, as visualised in the case of AIDS response programme. Many seek scapegoats like refugees, minorities, and the socially excluded, making it much harder for them to access the test and treatment of the virus. Donor nations will turn inward, feeling that they cannot afford to support others, as the presence of COVID-19 is a danger to people everywhere. It will not only harm developing countries but it will also affect donor countries (World Economic Forum, 2020). Every nation is learning from the present crisis brought about by COVID-19. Despite repeated warnings by the WHO on initial inaction, subsequent slow reactions and lack of consensus agreements of neighbouring countries indicate that the position of agencies set up in the past would need to be re-analysed precisely to avoid situations such as the present one (Shrestha et al., 2020).

Burden of Re-emergence and Re-infection

Even in normal times, half of the world's population is struggling or finds it difficult to afford basic healthcare services. In low-income nations, average health spending is just 41 dollars per person per year that can be annually estimated for 70 times less than that of countries with high incomes. The International Labour Organisation (ILO) estimates that 5 to 25 million jobs will be eradicated and 860 billion dollars to 3.4 trillion dollars in labour income will be lost globally. Furthermore, mass impoverishment would render health care treatment for many which is unavailable and one billion people are now barred from annual health coverage fees (Donthu et al., 2020). The World Health Organisation, which is considered the only global health organisation, officially promotes global health and combating global health crises is only as powerful and effective as its members want it to be. But the global burden in terms of health care responsibilities has led to many criticisms. Therefore, criticism of its position in managing COVID-19 needs to be measured (Bernes et al., 2020). The first wave analysis of COVID-19 was a devastating threat for humankind as many innocent lives have been swiped out. The burden of the first wave was bearable to some extent but it will not be the same for the second wave because global social thinkers predict that if COVID-19 re-emerges, then the complete threat to humankind can occur in a shorter span of time (CIDRAP, 2020). The re-emergence and re-infection of the virus, which can be also termed as the second wave, should be highly focused with due care and precaution as there have been examples of many re-emergence and re-infected cases from the recovered cases that have been recorded by the global health care institutions for their references (Duggan et al., 2020). Thus, the possibility of a global economic collapse and the advancement of health care systems will become a question to be answered by global institutions and local governments. Many developing and under developed nations have sustained to its maximum but re-emergence and re-infection without proper ailment and precautionary measures may make the situation difficult than before, causing lives and livelihoods to suffer (Nicola et al., 2020 and Nomani et al., 2020).

Challenges, Leadership, and Governance Response

COVID-19 has posed a huge challenge to the health systems, economies, and governments around the world. Leaders are under pressure in the midst of unprecedented difficulties and instability. Personal tragedies have reached to appropriate decisions which are to be handled for the immediate effects of the pandemic and its consequences for years to come (World Economic Forum, 2020). In order to fight against the virus, leaders around the world must unite and collectively work for better and immediate recovery. COVID-19, on the other hand, has also tested the potentiality of world leaders' governance and competence. Through proper cooperation and coordination between global nations and leaders, it becomes very essential and easy to overcome a crisis of this kind. There should be cooperation on research and knowledge, maintaining global supply, and warning about future outbreaks. This is to be shared through networking between nations (ICM, 2017). On the other hand, shutting down trade, acquiring products or preventing supply to other nations, closing borders, and tearing up international laws would make it harder to resume trade and travel (UNCTAD, 2020). An adaptable and successful practice followed, to control this virus, should be to broadcast globally in order to avoid territorial impacts of COVID-19. It can be expected that after the COVID-19 pandemic, future public investments by international agencies and global and local governments will have an allocation and importance duly for the public health and research, focusing on innovations and inventions majorly on the public health concern (OECD, 2020).

Majority of the sustainable development goals focus on the health care management, directly or indirectly, as there is still a lapse in ensuring good health and wellbeing (Sustainable Development Report, 2020). Looking on the response measures by various governments like that of the developed nations such as US and European countries, they have experienced pandemic to the worst as compared to the developing nations. The lack of awareness and inexperienced administrative actions have made the global nations suffer on a multidimensional point of view. It is already recorded from previous pandemics that sudden global changes especially on health crisis may encounter difficulties among world nations (CIDRAP, 2020). The formation of the G20 summit, which is a premier forum for the economic corporation, has also been a failure in predicting global crises on health, food, vaccine, etc. In order to prevent worst-case scenarios, current and future global threats need much better international coordination and far more decisive actions (Sustainable Development Report, 2020).

Implications and Country Experiences

The United Nations has called the COVID-19 pandemic as one of the greatest tests on humankind. This is much more than a global health emergency rather a systematic crisis that is already affecting economies and societies in unparalleled ways (UNDP, 2020). Most countries have responded with social distancing and lockdown measures. Economic and other activities have been severely diminished (Cheval et al., 2020). In the midst of this visceral epidemic, the tools and measures used to fight the disease are becoming painful and the pandemic has demonstrated not only how far the planet is from successful and cohesive global governance but also a crisis of trust in the institutions required to direct international action (Bernes et al., 2020).

The effectiveness of facemasks, lockdowns, social distancing, etc., have been globally accepted by people with due discipline in many of the nations as it has become a lifesaving agent. Social scientists have cautioned nations and the governments that there is a high possible uplift in domestic violence, child abuse, starvation for basic needs, and mental health crises. Family dynamics play a key role in deciding the implications for the crisis. Governments across nations must render their best to address these crises caused due to the pandemic, in family settings, to reduce the crime (World Economic Forum, 2020, OECD, 2020 and Branick, 2020).

In particular, politicians fear circumstances in which they have to adapt to fast-moving events and decide on policies without understanding the impacts and severity of the COVID-19 pandemic. If things go wrong, they will be blamed and even their government can be ignored by people (Lai, 2012). Failure to predict and plan for relevant international developments is leading to the erosion of global governance values and institutions. The natural response seems to turn inward on a domestic level and away from global cooperation. Global experts' foresight should raise awareness among policymakers for significant future changes with available policy options, in advance. A significant contribution to making global governance more risky, sensitive, and eventually successful will be experimenting and practicing with more resilient and sustainable approaches to globalisation (Bernes et al., 2020 and ICM, 2017). Human Development Report 2020 through advancing and reducing inequalities explains about a world grappling with unresolved contradictions is struck by the systemic crisis of COVID-19 between people and technology, between people and the Earth, and between the haves and the have-nots, all of which is supposed to form a new wave of disparities. The response to the crisis, however, is an opportunity to re-imagine a country's past and present experiences and come with a prepared solution to handle those tensions in the upcoming future (UNDP, 2020).

High Priority Areas and Action for Preventing Future Waves of COVID-19

The occurrence of this pandemic crisis has triggered nations across the world to concentrate on public health. The right approach towards crisis management teaches nations many positive and negative lessons to be learnt for the future (Sustainable Development Report, 2020). Guidelines about how to handle potential disasters should be re-established by the United Nations and World Health Organization (WHO). After the pandemic subsides, it is necessary to consolidate and evaluate the various experiences of each country in order to form a detailed set of lessons learnt from COVID-19 (Bernes et al., 2020). Humanity has learnt from many previous life threatening events, including wars and natural calamities, and has prioritised itself on preventive measures. A collective responsibility in the areas of health care on acute and chronic diseases can provide a holistic well-being of life (The Foundational Economic Collective, 2020).

Minorities, disadvantaged, and vulnerable sections of the society have many problems to be met in a normal life style. Thinking about the pandemic and its effects on their existence for survival is put forth as a question to the world's nations. Specific reservations and amenities should be ensured to these sections with due care at earliest (OAS/CIM, 2020). Various government agencies and health care organisations must ensure protection for the professionals who work on the field areas with the cases, on a worst case scenario like shortage of vaccine or heard immunity, a strategically recovery plan of action should be kept on high alert (CIDRAP, 2020 and OSHA, 2009). Priorities towards climate change and environment need to be included for action response as it is predicted that, between 2030 and 2050, the fatality will be approximately 250,000 excluding the death results due to communicable and non-communicable diseases. Migration, urbanisation and displacement can introduce new illnesses within human and animal interface (ICM, 2017).

Global epidemiologists are on alert after the first wave which came like a volcanic eruption in different locations. The world cannot exist in a perpetual lockdown so, working together, sharing medical information, and ensuring universal access to health is the only alternative to overcome this global crisis intervention (World Economic Forum, 2020). Crisis management analysis is in orientation and transformative of objective on fundamentally different foundations, embodies distinct behaviours, policies and perspectives, seeks alternative ends, and follows alternative processes (Branicki, 2020). Policy makers need to concentrate on mitigating the impact of health systems that will soon be overwhelmed (Prem et al., 2020). Lack of policies and ineffective response action by major international political bodies, in coping with the efforts and resources of COVID-19, with the expertise, access and demonstrated capacity to respond rapidly to developing events should be channelled. The transparency in accountability reflected and reinforced by the current international response to COVID-19 should be enhanced (Bernes et al., 2020).

Policy Relevance

Universal health care is a basic right of every person and investment for that component by nations around the world should be considered essential for humankind, looking forward to the well-being of every individual (Donthu et al., 2020). This crisis has taught the nations and policy makers a lesson on the possibilities of risk transfer mechanism including public and private sectors of managing their financial crisis and rebuilding their financial recovery (Gousseff et al., 2020). This global crisis has convincingly projected on disaster analysis, diplomacy on climate change, and ecosystem services to be re-think their strategic and integrated growth. Taking into account even the most unlikely events like the COVID-19 pandemic will inevitably recognise significant shifts in social and economic behaviour (Cheval et al., 2020).

A requirement in decisive action to ensure that the World Health Organisation and other globally recognised special health care institutions must collaborate, with national and local governments efficiently, and in a concerted manner regarding the global health system (ECDC, 2020). The national and local governments have a responsibility towards their countries' future, especially on its population, requiring commitments which sustain for an inclusive human development (Sustainable Development Report, 2020). The World Health Organisation has a responsibility to recognise and resolve the preparedness gaps found in the Global Health Security Index (WHO Interim Guidelines, 2007) which should be monitored comprehensively for both warning signs and the compliance of national governments with international obligations (Lai,2012). The monitored assessment should be re-examined periodically establishing rapid concerted action to counter any future pandemic crisis (Vora et al., 2020).

Many countries have suffered to their possible extent and regarding the future, the international financial institutions should plan emergency economic packages, especially those between highest and lowest economic countries (Ito, 2020). The most critical aspects of overcoming adversity are unity, openness, and international cooperation (Dodds et al., 2020). There is a need to strengthen national and sub-national regarding the concerned areas to disadvantaged communities and reinforce inclusiveness on the recovery process, support systems, and well-targeted services through identifying needs for equalisation of policies (OECD, 2020). Though there have been a number of emerging studies in this field, it is clear that the pandemic has created a multifaceted response among the professionals worldwide, even though the quality of evidence and literature background is relatively low. The observations and suggestions from the global experts and professionals have been considered and recorded in this paper through various available sources. Though there are many barriers and difficulties in managing the impacts of this pandemic, there is a need for further research, from eminent researchers and local institutions across the world, about causes and impacts of COVID-19 on an multidimensional point of view such that solutions for the crisis can be estimated with due inference.

References

[1] L. Branicki (July 03, 2020). *COVID-19, Ethics of Care and Feminist Crisis Management*. John Willy and Sons Limited. Accessed on January 25, 2021, retrieved from https://onlinelibrary.wiley.com/doi/10.1111/gwao.12491

[2] C. Giacomo, C. Corentin, S. Francesco (2020). *Second Wave COVID-19 Pandemics in Europe: A Temporal Playbook*. Scientific Report, Nature Research. Accessed on January 25, 2021, retrieved from https://arxiv.org/pdf/2007.13100.pdf

[3] Center for Disease Control and prevention (CDC), April, 2017. *Get Your School Ready for Pandemic Flu*. U.S. Department of Health and Human Services. Accessed on January 25, 2021, retrieved from https://www.cdc.gov/nonpharmaceutical-interventions/pdf/gr-pan-flu-ed-set.pdf

[4] S. Cheval, C. Mihai Adamescu, T. Georgiadis, M. Herrnegger, A. Piticar, and D. Legates, June 10, 2020. *Observed and Potential Impacts of the COVID-19 Pandemic on the Environment*. Accessed on January 26, 2021, retrieved from https://www.mdpi.com/1660-4601/17/11/4140

[5] Committee for the Coordination of Statistical Activities (CCSA). *How COVID-19 is Changing the World: A Statistical Perspective*. Volume I October 07, 2020. Accessed on January 25, 2021, retrieved from https://data.unicef.org/resources/how-covid-19-is-changing-the-world-a-statistical-perspective/

[6] *COVID-19 – CIDRAP Viewpoint*, University of Minnesota. April 30, 2020. Accessed on January 25, 2021, retrieved from https://www.cidrap.umn.edu/sites/default/files/public/downloads/cidrap-covid19-viewpoint-part1_0.pdf

[7] D.L. Heymann and N. Shindo, February 22, 2020. *COVID-19: What is Next for Public Health?* The Lancet, vol 395. Accessed on January 26, 2021, retrieved from https://www.thelancet.com/journals/lancet/article/PIIS0140-6736(20)30374-3/fulltext

[8] D.M. Hartley and Perencevich E.N., May 19, 2020. *Public Health Interventions for COVID-19*. Accessed on January 26, 2021, retrieved from https://jamanetwork.com/journals/jama/fullarticle/2764656

[9] N. Donthu and A. Gustafsson, June 09, 2020. *Effects of COVID-19 on Business and Research*. Accessed on January 26, 2021, retrieved from https://www.sciencedirect.com/science/article/pii/S0148296320303830

[10] N. Duggan, S. Ludy, B. Shannon, A. Reisner, and S. Wilcox, July 04, 2020. *Is Novel Coronavirus 2019 Reinfection Possible? Interpreting Dynamic SARS-CoV-2 Test Results*. Accessed on January 26, 2021, retrieved from https://www.sciencedirect.com/science/article/pii/S0735675720305830

[11] European Center for Disease Prevention and Control (ECDC), September 21, 2020. *Reinfection with SARS-CoV-2 Considerations for Public Health Response*. Accessed on January 25, 2021, retrieved from https://www.ecdc.europa.eu/sites/default/files/documents/Re-infection-and-viral-shedding-threat-assessment-brief.pdf

[12] European Parliamentary Research Service (EPRS), February, 2020. *Economic Impact of Epidemics and Pandemics*. Accessed on January 25, 2021, retrieved from https://www.europarl.europa.eu/RegData/etudes/BRIE/2020/646195/EPRS_BRI(2020)646195_EN.pdf

[13] M. Gousseff, P. Penot, L. Gallay, D. Batisse, N. Benech, K. Bouiller, and E. Botelho-Nevers, June 30, 2020. *Clinical Recurrences of COVID-19 Symptoms After Recovery: Viral Relapse, Reinfection or Inflammatory Rebound?* Accessed on January 26, 2021, retrieved from https://www.sciencedirect.com/science/article/pii/S0163445320304540

[14] Independent Commission on Multilateralism (ICM), October, 2017. *Global Pandemics and Global Public Health.* Accessed on January 25, 2021, retrieved from https://www.worldcat.org/title/global-pandemics-and-global-public-health/oclc/1140990104

[15] International Labour Organisation (ILO), March 18, 2020. *COVID-19 and the World of Work: Impact and Policy Responses*. Monitor 1st Edition. Accessed on January 25, 2021, retrieved from http://www.ilo.org/wcmsp5/groups/public/---dgreports/---dcomm/documents/briefingnote/wcms_738753.pdf

[16] T. Ito, August 13, 2020. *Impact of the Coronavirus Pandemic Crisis on the Financial System in the Eurozone*. Accessed on January 26, 2021, retrieved from https://onlinelibrary.wiley.com/doi/abs/10.1002/jcaf.22466?af=R

[17] K. Dodds, V.C. Broto, K. Detterbeck, M. Jones, V. Mamadouh, M. Ramutsindela, M. Varsanyi, D. Wachsmuth, and C. YuanWoon, 2020. *The COVID-19 Pandemic: Territorial, Political and Governance Dimensions of the Crisis, Territory, Politics, Governance*, 8: 3, pp. 289-298. Accessed on January 26, 2021, retrieved from https://doi.org/10.1080/21622671.2020.1771022

[18] A. Lai, 2012. *Organisational Collaborative Capacity in Fighting Pandemic Crises: A Literature Review from the Public Management Perspective*. Asia Pacific Journal of Public Health. SAGE Publications. Accessed on January 26, 2021, retrieved from https://journals.sagepub.com/doi/10.1177/1010539511429592

[19] M. Vora, C. Barikar, M., R. Bhattacharyya, 2020. *Worried Well and COVID-19: Re-emergence of an Old Quandary*. Asian Journal of Psychiatry.

Accessed on January 26, 2021, retrieved from https://www.sciencedirect.com/journal/asian-journal-of-psychiatry/vol/54/suppl/C

[20] Md. Z.M. Nomani, Rehana Parveen, January 01, 2020. *Legal Dimensions of Public Health with Special Reference to COVID-19 Pandemic in India*. Accessed on January 26, 2021, retrieved from http://www.sysrevpharm.org/?mno=121024

[21] M. Muller, A. Boudet, and I. Gaddis, April 16, 2020. *Gender Dimensions of the COVID-19 Pandemic*. World Bank Group. Policy Note. Accessed on January 25, 2021, retrieved from https://elibrary.worldbank.org/doi/abs/10.1596/33622

[22] M. Nicola, Z. Alsafi, C. Sohrabi, A. Kerwan, A. Al-Jabir, C. Iosifidis, R. Agha, April 17, 2020. *The Socio-economic Implications of the Coronavirus Pandemic (COVID-19): A Review*. Accessed on January 25, 2021, retrieved from https://www.sciencedirect.com/science/article/pii/S1743919120303162

[23] The Organization of American States/Inter American Commission of Women (OAS/CIM) May 1, 2020, *COVID-19 in Women's Lives: Reasons to Recognize the Differential Impacts – World 2020*. Inter-American Commission for Women. Accessed on January 25, 2021, retrieved from https://reliefweb.int/report/world/covid-19-women-s-lives-reasons-recognize-differential-impacts

[24] Occupational Safety and Health Administration (OSHA), 2009 *Pandemic Influenza Preparedness and Response Guidance for Healthcare Workers and Healthcare Employees*. Accessed on January 27, 2021, retrieved from https://www.osha.gov/Publications/3328-05-2007-English.html

[25] The Organization for Economic Co-operation and Development (OECD), June 16, 2020. *The Territorial Impact of COVID-19: Managing the Crisis Across Levels of Government. Tackling Coronavirus (Covid-19) Contributing to a Global Effort*. Accessed on January 25, 2021, retrieved from http://www.oecd.org/coronavirus/policy-responses/the-territorial-impact-of-covid-19-managing-the-crisis-across-levels-of-government-d3e314e1/

[26] M. Pennington, July 29, 2020. *Hayek on Complexity, Uncertainty and Pandemic Response*. The Review of Austrian Economics. Springer Journals. Accessed on January 25, 2021, retrieved from https://www.researchgate.net/publication/343317113_Hayek_on_complexity_uncertainty_and_pandemic_response

[27] K. Prem, Y. Liu, T.W. Russell, A.J. Kucharski, R.M. Eggo, N. Davies, M. Jit, P. Klepac, March 25, 2020. *The Effect of Control Strategies to Reduce Social Mixing on Outcomes of the COVID-19 Epidemic in Wuhan, China: A Modelling Study*. Retrieved January 26, 2021, from https://pubmed.ncbi.nlm.nih.gov/32220655/

[28] Sustainable Development Report, June, 2020. *The Sustainable Development Goals and Covid-19*. Cambridge University Press. Accessed on January 25, 2021, retrieved from https://sdgindex.org/reports/sustainable-development-report-2020/

[29] The Foundational Economic Collective, August 18, 2020. *What Comes After Pandemic. COVID-19 Ten Point Platform for Foundational Renewal*. The Foundational Economic Collective. Accessed on January 25, 2021, retrieved from https://foundationaleconomy.com/covid-19-report/

[30] T. Bernes, L. Brozus, M. Hatuel-Radoshitzky, A. Heistein, E. Greco, P. Sas-nal, I. Yurgens, S. Kulik, Y. Turianskyi, S. Gruzd, E. Sidiropoulos, N. Grobbelaar, S. Yenel, C.J. Regazzoni, C. Dongxiao, L. Chuanying, K. Kapur, S. Suri, P. Vermonte, Y.R. Damuri, S. Muhibat, and M. Ca-ballero-Anthony, May, 2020. *Challenges of Global Governance Amid the COVID-19 Pandemic*. Council on Foreign Relations, International institutions and Global Governance program. Accessed on January 26, 2021, retrieved from https://cdn.cfr.org/sites/default/files/report_pdf/challenges-of-global-governance-amid-the-covid-19-pandemic.pdf

[31] United Nations Development Programme (UNDP), Human Development Reports, 2020. *COVID-19 and Human Development, Assessing the Crisis, Envisioning the Recovery*. Accessed on January 25, 2021, retrieved from http://hdr.undp.org/en/hdp-covid

[32] United National Conference on Trade and Development (UNCTAD), 2020. *Covid-19 and Tourism: Assessing the Economic Consequences*. Accessed on January 25, 2021, retrieved from https://unctad.org/webflyer/covid-19-and-tourism-assessing-economic-consequences

[33] United Nations Comprehensive Response (UN) to COVID-19: *Saving Lives, Protecting Societies, Recovering Better*, June, 2020. Accessed on January 25, 2021, retrieved from https://www.un.org/sites/un2.un.org/files/un_comprehensive_response_to_covid-19_june_2020.pdf

[34] WHO Interim Guidelines, June, 2007. *Infection Prevention and Control of Epidemic- and Pandemic-prone Acute Respiratory Diseases in Health Care*. Accessed on January 25, 2021, retrieved from https://apps.who.int/iris/bitstream/handle/10665/69707/WHO_CDS_EPR_2007.6_eng.pdf?sequence=1

[35] World Economic Forum, May, 2020. *Challenges and Opportunities in the Post-COVID-19 World*. Accessed on January 25, 2021, retrieved from https://www.weforum.org/reports/post-covid-19-challenges-and-opportunities

CHAPTER 3

Mental Health and Challenges of Healthcare Workers during the Outbreak of COVID-19 Epidemic in India

Udhayakumar P.[1], **Sigamani Panneer**[2], **Robert Ramesh Babu P.**[3] and **G. Josiah Stanely Rose**[4]

Abstract: *Healthcare workers are first-line warriors handling patients with COVID-19. Each day, they encounter a high risk of being contaminated and are expected to work for long hours. Maladaptive coping, lack of training, and lack of social support are significant risk factors related to mental health disorders among healthcare workers. An increase in the number of confirmed and suspected cases, overwork, lack of personal protective equipment, widespread media attention, and lack of particular medications may all contribute to the emotional strain of these healthcare personnel. Responding to the spread of COVID-19, healthcare personnel in India reported significant rates of depression, anxiety, sleeplessness, and discomfort. Recognizing the mental health reactions to a public health crisis may aid healthcare providers, and communities prepare for a disaster's response. Proper assimilation of mental health issues would help the professionals to prepare themselves to cope with the COVID-19 disaster. Therefore, it is essential to study medical workers' mental health status. Studies exploring the mental health problems among healthcare professionals during the COVID-19 outbreak in India are limited. This paper aims to highlight the mental health problems, occupational health, and*

[1] Assistant Professor, The Department of Social Work, Central University of Tamil Nadu, Thiruvarur, India. E-mail: pudhayakumar@cutn.ac.in

[2] Professor and Head, The School of Social Sciences and Humanities, The Department of Social Work, Central University of Tamil Nadu, Thiruvarur, India. E-mail: sigamanip@cutn.ac.in

[3] Ph.D. Scholar, Department of Social Work, School of Social Sciences and Humanities, Central University of Tamil Nadu, Thiruvarur, India. E-mail: robertrb19@students.cutn.ac.in

[4] Ph.D. Scholar, The School of Social Sciences and Humanities, The Department of Social Work, Central University of Tamil Nadu, Thiruvarur, India. E-mail: josiahstanelyrose@gmail.com

challenges faced by healthcare professionals during the COVID-19 pandemic and suggest suitable interventions to address the mental health needs of these professionals in India. Moreover, this might help the public healthcare system recognize the causes of the mental health issues among healthcare workers and provide effective intervention to face the challenges posed by COVID-19.

Keywords: COVID-19, Occupational Health, Healthcare Workers, Mental Health, Pandemic

Introduction

The COVID-19 outbreak is a pandemic, and coronavirus has been known as the origin of an outbreak of respiratory illness (WHO, 2020). The World Health Organisation convened an emergency meeting on January 30, 2020, and proclaimed the worldwide COVID-19 outbreak of international concern as a public health emergency (WHO, 2020). Faced with this crucial situation, front-line healthcare providers are undergoing mental health issues as they are directly involved in the care of COVID-19 patients (Lai et al., 2020). Medical personnel is the first line of defense in incidents involving COVID-19. Every day, they confront a significant risk of infection and are subjected to lengthy and stressful work shifts to satisfy health criteria (Fava et al., 2019). On 20 January 2020, there were 282 confirmed cases with six fatalities, which increased to 5,49,11,612 confirmed cases with 13,25,346 deaths from over 220 nations and territories by 15 November 2020. The United States has been the worst-hit country, followed by India and Brazil. The infection spread at an alarming rate. With about 1.38 billion people, India is the world's second-most populous country and the biggest in South Asia. As a result, the danger of probable diseases and fatalities is greater. Lockdowns, curfews, emergency-like conditions, border closures, extensive airport inspections, quarantines, and physical separation have all become the new normal throughout the world. India reported 34,555,431 confirmed cases on 22 November 2021, as shown in Table 1.

During the COVID-19 outbreak, medical health workers have had psychosocial problems (Zang et al., 2020). Healthcare personnel who care for individuals infected with COVID-19 experience emotional stress, physical strain, separation from families, shame, and the anguish of losing patients and colleagues. Frontline medical personnel are vulnerable to the physical and psychological consequences of COVID-19 (Adams and Walls, 2020). The growing number of confirmed and suspected cases,

Table 1: India COVID-19 Statistics

Timeline	*Total Confirmed Cases*	*Total Deaths*
11 January 2021	10,557,985	152,274
8 February 2021	10,904,940	155,642
15 March 2021	11,599,130	159,755
12 April 2021	14,788,109	177,150,
10 May 2021	24,684,077	270,284
14 June 2021	29,881,965	386,713
12 July 2021	31,106,065	413,225
9 August 2021	32,192,576	431,225
13 September 2021	33,448,163	444,838
11 October 2021	34,667,719	452,124
22 November 2021	34,555,431	467,468

Source: https://www.worldometers.info/coronavirus/country/india/ (accessed on 23rd November 2021)

demanding workload, depletion of PPE, broad media attention, shortage of particular medications, and emotions of being under-supported may all add to the emotional stress of this health care personnel (Lai et al., 2020). Other than patients, healthcare professionals are isolated and anxious about going back home and perhaps being a source of infection to the other members of their families (Mohindra et al., 2020). They go through heavy workloads and mental pressure. Moreover, they are at risk of moral injury. The outbreak of COVID-19 has caused unusual public health concerns and enormous mental health problems amongst health care professionals. It has affected their grasping power, concentration, decision-making skills, and well-being.

Recognizing the mental health reactions to a public health crisis may aid health care providers and communities in preparing for a disaster's response. Proper assimilation of mental health issues would help professionals cope with the COVID-19 disaster. Therefore, it is essential to study medical workers' mental health status (Kang et al., 2020). Studies exploring mental health problems among healthcare professionals during the COVID-19 outbreak in India are limited. This paper aims to highlight mental health problems, occupational stress, and challenges faced by the healthcare professionals during the COVID-19 pandemic and suggest suitable interventions to address the mental health needs of healthcare professionals in India. Moreover, this might help the public health care recognise the causes of mental health issues among health care workers and provide effective intervention to face the challenges posed by COVID-19.

Mental Health Problems Among Health Care Professionals

Healthcare workers are at the risk of not just adverse physical outcomes of coronavirus but also psychological (Gold, 2020). Evidence from previous pandemics suggests that healthcare professionals may have symptoms of post-traumatic stress disorder, depression, and drug use problems. Preliminary data from China and Italy during the COVID-19 pandemic offer further evidence that healthcare workers in China reported depression (50.3 per cent), anxiety (44.6 per cent, and insomnia (34.0 per cent) (Lai et al., 2019). The growing risk factors associated with mental health problems among healthcare workers include maladaptive coping and lack of training and social support (Naushad et al., 2019). An increase in the number of confirmed and suspected cases, overwork, lack of personal protective equipment (PPE), widespread media attention, and lack of particular medications may all contribute to the emotional strain of this healthcare personnel (Lai et al., 2020). Previous studies have reported that healthcare workers fear of infection of their family, friends, and colleagues (Maunder et al., 2003), feel uncertainty and stigmatization (Bai et al., 2004), have reported job hesitancy and high levels of stress, worry, and depression symptoms which might have long-term psychological consequences (Lee et al., 2004). Personal caregiving and socioeconomic pressures such as having children at home, having an infected family member, and having a low family income, were linked to worse mental health outcomes among healthcare workers (Kisely et al., 2020). Experiences during the Ebola virus outbreak suggest that healthcare workers experience incredibly high stress (Mohammed et al., 2015). In the case of COVID-19-related stress, healthcare workers are expected to have symptoms like preoccupation with the risks of COVID-19, compulsive attention to COVID-19-related news, insomnia, anxiety, guilt, grief, avoidance of turning back to the healthcare setting, irritability, nightmares, and depression. In many others, these symptoms will get resolved without intervention. However, these symptoms may add to burnout and functional impairment among healthcare workers (Krystal and McNeil, 2020). The frontline workers are under the continuous stress of getting a viral infection while working in a hospital setting with sparsely available PPE, rising work demands, apprehension about transmitting the disease to their family members. Addressing the mental health needs of healthcare workers was an essential component of the public health system in India during the COVID-19 outbreak. Appropriate interventions to enhance the mental well-being of healthcare workers exposed to COVID-19 need to be implemented immediately.

Occupational Health of Healthcare Workers Amid COVID-19 Pandemic

On World Safety and Health at Work Day, the World Health Organisation (WHO) urged all governments, employers, workers' groups, and the global community to take the essential steps to increase nations' capacity to safeguard occupational health and the safety of healthcare professionals. Amid the COVID-19 pandemic, International Labour Organisation (ILO) has dedicated the World Day for Safety and Health at Work (2020) to address the outbreak of infectious diseases at workplaces, specifically the COVID-19 pandemic. Healthcare professionals are exposed to a high-risk infection, overstressed due to extended duty hours, and troubled due to a lack of proper ways of controlling the pandemic. Infection prevention requires all healthcare personnel to practice effective infection prevention and control techniques, emphasizing hand cleanliness and PPE use while caring for COVID-19 patients. Healthcare workers affected by COVID-19 should have the right to get employment injury compensations for occupational disease, including rehabilitation and curative services (ILO, 2020). Moreover, the World Health Organisation has urged governments, companies, and labor groups to implement zero-tolerance policies for workplace violence against healthcare professionals (WHO, 2020).

Challenges of Healthcare Workers during the COVID-19 Pandemic

There is a lack of essential PPE, medical facilities, space to accommodate patients, and testing kits. This creates difficulty for healthcare professionals to carry out their duties and affects their mental health. They are mostly emotionally affected when many COVID-19 patients do not survive, despite clinical care (Alradhawi et al., 2020). They are also affected by broader societal and economic tensions, including the impacts of social distancing and fewer social resources (Trac et al., 2020). Healthcare workers in COVID wards face unprecedented challenges while delivering healthcare services. According to Kang et al. (2020), the significant challenges faced by healthcare workers during the COVID-19 pandemic are lack of PPE, lack of clarity regarding indications for its use, intense scrutiny of international media, isolation from family, fear of spreading the virus to family members, rapidly growing workload with an increasing number of suspected and confirmed cases, and progressively depleting workforce to deal with a growing amount of suspected and confirmed cases. When coping with the issues of the COVID-19 pandemic, healthcare workers are at a higher risk of moral harm. Though moral injury is not considered a mental illness, it can lead to negative thoughts, feelings of guilt, shame, or disgust among healthcare workers (Greenberg et al., 2020). The challenges faced by healthcare workers in India are shortage of PPE, long working hours, violence, increased risk of infection to the family members, social and family impacts (Vaishya, 2020). Most healthcare facilities in India face a shortage of PPE, including face masks, gowns, and respirators. Both hospitals lack these things are highly-priced due to the increasing demand. Healthcare professionals' long duty hours have adversely affected their physical and mental health.

The COVID-19 outbreak has influenced stressful job conditions in many ways. Being assigned to unfamiliar tasks was stressful for some healthcare workers. Change in the workload over time was associated with a higher stress level. Many healthcare workers had difficulty going back home, especially children present at home. Besides, health workers with children experience a higher level of distress. Stigma is another challenge experienced by healthcare workers, which is considered a significant predictor of burnout and fatigue ach et al., 2020). Stigmatization among healthcare workers is associated with physical and mental health. Healthcare workers who have experienced higher stigmatization report having increased psychological distress and a certain amount of increased somatic symptoms (Corrigan and Gallagher, 2015). Healthcare workers who are predicted to face higher levels of stigma report higher levels of psychological discomfort, which may be crucial in predicting the influence on healthcare workers' outcomes (Corrigan and Gallagher, 2015). Working with potentially highly contagious individuals causes a great deal of stigma (Arnold, 2003). The social isolation experienced by healthcare workers included the fear that people avoided contact with them or their families. Healthcare workers are at high risk of violence across the globe. Studies found that between 8 per cent and 38 per cent of health workers encounter physical violence in their workplace once in their lifetime. Furthermore, individuals have been intimidated or subjected to verbal abuse and social humiliation due to their work. During the COVID-19 crisis, a lack of staff and resources and rising societal tensions led to an upsurge in violence against healthcare professionals and even assaults in healthcare institutions (WHO, 2020).

Promoting the Happiness of Healthcare Workers at Workplaces

Happy employees are more prolific at work, and happiness is critical for productivity and skill retention. Since healthcare workers are at significant risk of adverse mental health consequences during the COVID-19 outbreak (Rajkumar, 2020), lifestyle-based mind development programs can bring about happiness in their workplace, increasing productivity and enhancing healthcare quality services (Gunathunga, 2016). To reduce the risk of developing mental health problems, the following interventions can be utilized to achieve happiness among healthcare workers at their workplaces: mobile apps like Breath2Relax, Headspace, MoodGYm, and stress Gym can be used for relaxation and meditation (Bansal et al., 2020), establishing a health surveillance system for healthcare professionals would help in the early detection of problems and timely intervention can be given (Bolier et al., 2014), and using self-compassion as an intervention can improve the happiness of healthcare professionals (Neff et al., 2007). Mindfulness training programmes like mindfulness-based therapy, self-compassion, gratitude meditation, and yoga practices can help healthcare professionals enhance happiness (Hedderman, 2020). Healthcare professionals have to incorporate self-care as a culture (Gengoux, 2018). Positive interventions like 'Three Good Things, which involves writing down three good things that happened during the shift and passing it to the next batch of healthcare professionals or writing down the 'Awesome Moments' and sharing them with other healthcare professionals, can be helpful practices (Parsons, 2008). Moreover, Stress Management and Resilience Training program (SMART) as an intervention can enhance happiness among healthcare workers (Berkland, 2017).

Intervention Strategies for Healthcare Workers

This article affirms that psychosocial and workplace measures can improve employees' working lives and mental well-being. Access to sufficient PPE, enough rest, and psychological support is associated with favorable psychological outcomes with healthcare workers (Kisely et al., 2020). Using psychological first aid to reduce risk, a specific psychological intervention can be provided depending on the requirements of a particular health professional. Proper assimilation of mental health issues would help professionals prepare themselves to cope with the COVID-19 disaster (Keudell et al., 2016). Considering the unprecedented challenges faced by the general population and healthcare workers in dealing with the novel coronavirus in India, the National Institute of Mental Health and Neuroscience (NIMHANS) developed guidelines for effective mental health management in general medical and specialized mental healthcare settings and also address safety issues of psychiatrists and other healthcare providers. It stresses the importance of self-care practices. Furthermore, team leaders should reduce mental health issues, and administrators should be aware that mental health assistance is a critical component of the COVID-19 response. Frontline personnel needs to be trained in simple and emerging evidence-based assessment and management strategies. Besides, digital-enabled learning and support for mental health issues need to be considered for all non-psychiatric medical professionals and frontline personnel (Murthy, 2020). Since the frontline workers need specialized care to assure high-quality service delivery, a helpline assigned to them might enable prompt attention to their mental health problems.

Healthcare workers serving in COVID wards are at high risk of viral infection. They may also experience guilt and fear that they may have infected their team, family members, and other patients. It is vital that employees in quarantine feel supported by their close co-workers. Team leaders must ensure that employees who are quarantined have frequent social interaction (Thamby and Jaisoorya, 2020). The Workplace catastrophically impacts healthcare workers' well-being due to longer working shifts. They need to be educated to use proper coping strategies to overcome this stress (Holmes et al., 2019). In India, there have been rising levels of violence against healthcare workers (Lancet, 2020). Doctors, nurses, security staff, and others involved in testing, tracing contacts and imposing physical distancing measures to combat COVID-19 have experienced threats and harassment. As a result, the World Health Organisation urges governments, companies, and labor groups to implement zero-tolerance policies for violence against healthcare personnel. Healthcare workers may also face moral injury, leading to negative thoughts, feelings of guilt, shame, or disgust. As a result, healthcare practitioners must be prepared for the ethical problems during the COVID-19 epidemic. Researchers specializing in psychiatry, behavioral and social science, digital healthcare providers, policymakers, and other stakeholders must collaborate to develop innovative and practical technologies to address the mental health needs of healthcare workers during the current pandemic and prepare healthcare workers to address similar health challenges in future outbreaks. Given the anticipated findings, such research will likely strengthen advocacy efforts to promote the mental well-being of healthcare workers. Moreover, research studies can explore how enhance then and monitor the mental health conditions of healthcare professionals (Xing et al., 2020). Since the pandemic will continue, good health policies and strategies have to be developed involving mental health professionals.

- Implement national and local level initiatives and programmes to promote frontline healthcare workers' well-being based on evidence-based practices.
- We need to utilize the experience of health and behavioral science specialists to guide solutions.
- Distribute and share these resources throughout institutions, a network of partners, patients, and others.
- Condemn and fight the stigmatization of front-line healthcare professionals. Increase efforts to de-stigmatize mental health in society as a whole.
- Promote a broader and more actionable conversation about mental health in the workplace.
- Involve frontline healthcare workers in government decisions and formulation of new policies.
- Create national knowledge bases (information, tools, and resources) to meet the requirements of workers and their leaders in times of crisis, recovery, and rebuilding.
- Consider the possibility for digital technology and other creative techniques to help and train the healthcare workforce.
- Maintain sufficient staff levels in healthcare systems and fair remuneration for workers.
- Encourage help-seeking and make mental health options available to frontline healthcare professionals in distress.
- Healthcare professionals need to be appreciated for their dedicated services to help humanity.
- At an individual, organizational, and societal level, world leaders and other decision-makers must find ways to invest in the overall well-being of the healthcare staff.

Conclusion

Healthcare workers encounter considerable challenges during the outbreak of the COVID-19 pandemic. Ensuring the health and safety of healthcare workers will shape the pandemic in India, thus affecting its long-run impacts on social stability, economic growth, and security. Adequate PPE provided by the hospitals is considered the most crucial motivational factor that might encourage healthcare workers to continue their service. Continued acknowledgment of healthcare workers by the public health system and hospital management, framing infection control guidelines, specialized equipment, drawing up comprehensive public health policies, and encouraging timely research may reassure healthcare workers to work during the current COVID-19 pandemic with similar kinds of outbreaks in future.

References

[1] J.G. Adams, and R.M. Walls (2020). 'Supporting the Health Care Workforce during the Covid-19 Global Epidemic'. *Jama*, 323(15), pp.1439-1440.

[2] M. Alradhawi, N. Shubber, J. Sheppard, and Y. Ali (2020). Effects of the COVID-19 Pandemic on Mental Well-being Amongst Individuals in a Society – A Letter to the Editor on 'The Socio-Economic Implications of the Coronavirus and COVID-19 Pandemic: A Review'. *International journal of surgery* (London, England). Retrieved from https://doi.org/10.1016/j.ijsu.2020.04.070, Accessed on 16th October 2021

[3] Y. Bai, C. Lin, C., C. Lin, J. Chen, C.M. Chue, and P. Chou (2004). 'Survey of Stress Reactions Among Health Care Workers Involved with the SARS Outbreak'. *Psychiatric Services*, 55(9), pp.1055–1057. Retrieved from https://doi.org/10.1176/appi.ps.55.9.1055, Accessed on 14th July 2021

[4] L. Bolier, S.M. Ketelaar, K. Nieuwenhuijsen, O. Smeets, F.R. Gärtner, and J.K. Sluiter (2014). 'Workplace Mental Health Promotion Online to Enhance Well-being of Nurses and Allied Health Professionals: A Cluster-Randomized Controlled Trial'. *Internet interventions*, 1(4), pp.196-204.

[5] B.E. Berkland, B.L. Werneburg, S.M. Jenkins, J.L. Friend, M.M. Clark, J.K. Rosedahl, and A. Sood (2017). 'A Worksite Wellness Intervention: Improving Happiness, Life Satisfaction, and Gratitude in Health Care Workers'. *Mayo Clinic Proceedings: Innovations, Quality, and Outcomes*, 1(3), pp. 203–210.

[6] S.K. Brooks, R.K. Webster, L.E. Smith, L. Woodland, S. Wessely, N. Greenberg, and G.J. Rubin (2020). 'The Psychological Impact of Quarantine and How to Reduce It: A Rapid Review of the Evidence'. *The Lancet*, 395(10227), 912–920. https://doi.org/10.1016/S0140-6736(20)30460-8

[7] G.A. Fava, B.S. McEwen, J. Guidi, S. Gostoli, E. Offidani, and N. Sonino (2019). 'Clinical Characterization of Allostatic Overload'. *Psychoneuroendocrinology*. 108, 94-101, https://doi.org/10.1016/j.psyneuen.2019.05.028

[8] M.W. Gunathunga (2016). 'Improving Performance and Happiness Among Healthcare Workers Through a Body-Mind Approach in a Healthcare Setting in Sri Lanka'. *Work*, 55(2), pp. 305–309.

[9] G.W. Gengoux, and L.W. Roberts (2018). 'Enhancing Wellness and Engagement Among Healthcare Professionals'. *Acad Psychiatry*, pp. 42, 1–4.

[10] N. Greenberg, M. Docherty, S. Gnanapragasam, and S. Wessely (2020). 'Managing Mental Health Challenges Faced by Healthcare Workers during the Covid-19 Pandemic'. *BMJ*, 368.

[11] J.A. Gold (2020). 'Covid-19: Adverse Mental Health Outcomes for Healthcare Workers'. *BMJ*. https://doi.org/10.1136/bmj.m2491, accessed on 21st June 2021.

[12] E.A. Holmes, R.C. O'Connor, V.H. Perry, I. Tracey, S. Wessely, L. Arseneault, and T. Ford (2020). 'Multidisciplinary Research Priorities for The Covid-19 Pandemic: A Call for Action for Mental Health Science'. *The Lancet Psychiatry*, 7(6), 547–560.

[13] E. Hedderman, V. O'Doherty, and S. O'Connor (2020). 'Mindfulness Moments for Clinicians in the Midst of a Pandemic'. *Irish Journal of Psychological Medicine*, pp. 1–14.

[14] International Labour Organisation (2020). 'World Day for Safety and Health at Work 2020 – Stop the Pandemic: Safety and Health at Work can Save Lives'. Retrieved from https://www.ilo.org/global/topics/safety-and-health-at-work/events-training/events-meetings/world-day-safety-health-at-work/WCMS_739669/lang--en/index.htm, accessed on 22nd May 2021.

[15] A.M. Lee, J.G. Wong, G.M. McAlonan, V. Cheung, C. Cheung, P.C. Sham, and S.E. Chua (2007). 'Stress and Psychological Distress Among SARS Survivors One Year After the Outbreak'. *The Canadian Journal of Psychiatry*, 52(4), pp. 233-240.

[16] J. Lai, S. Ma, Y. Wang, Z. Cai, J. Hu, N. Wei, and H. Tan (2020). 'Factors Associated with Mental Health Outcomes Among Healthcare Workers Exposed to Coronavirus Disease 2019'. *JAMA network open*, 3(3), e203976-e203976. http://jamanetwork.com/article.aspx?doi=10.1001/jamanetworkopen.2020.3976 accessed on 7th July 2021.

[17] T. Lancet (2020). 'India under COVID-19 Lockdown'. *Lancet* (London, England), 395(10233), pp. 1315. https://dx.doi.org/10.1016%2FS0140-6736(20)30938-7 accessed on 25th July 2021.

[18] L. Kang, Y. Li, S. Hu, M. Chen, C. Yang, B.X. Yang, and J. Chen (2020). 'The Mental Health of Medical Workers in Wuhan, China, is Dealing with the 2019 Novel Coronavirus'. *The Lancet Psychiatry*, 7(3), e14. https://

psycnet.apa.org/doi/10.1016/S2215-0366(20)30047-X, accessed on 16th September 2021.

[19] S. Kisely, N. Warren, L. McMahon, C. Dalais, I. Henry, and D. Siskind (2020). 'Occurrence, Prevention, and Management of the Psychological Effects of Emerging Virus Outbreaks on Healthcare Workers: Rapid Review and Meta-analysis'. *BMJ*, 369. https://doi.org/10.1136/bmj.m1642, accessed on 2nd May 2021.

[20] J.H. Krystal, and R.L. McNeil (2020). 'Responding to the Hidden Pandemic for Healthcare Workers: Stress'. *Nature Medicine*, 26(5), pp. 639–639.

[21] R. Maunder, J. Hunter, L. Vincent, J. Bennett, N. Peladeau, M. Leszcz, and T. Mazzulli (2003). 'The Immediate Psychological and Occupational Impact of the 2003 SARS Outbreak in a Teaching Hospital'. *CMAJ*, 168(10), pp. 1245–1251.

[22] A. Mohammed, T.L. Sheikh, G. Poggensee, P. Nguku, A. Olayinka, C. Ohuabunwo, and J. Eaton (2015). 'Mental Health in Emergency Response: Lessons from Ebola'. *The Lancet Psychiatry*, 2(11), pp. 955–957.

[23] R. Mohindra, V. Suri, A. Bhalla, and S.M. Singh (2020). 'Issues Relevant to Mental Health Promotion in Frontline Health Care Providers Managing Quarantined/Isolated Covid-19 Patients'. *Asian Journal of Psychiatry*, 51(3), 102084, https://doi.org/10.1016/j.ajp.2020.102084, accessed on 8th September 2021.

[24] P. Murthy (2020). 'The COVID-19 Pandemic and Mental Health – An Introduction'. *Mental Health in the Times of COVID-19 Pandemic – Guidance for General Medical and Specialised Mental Health Care Settings*. Department of Psychiatry, NIMHANS.

[25] C.L. Parsons (2008). 'Positive Psychology and Positive Interventions for Nurses'. Retrieved from https://repository.upenn.edu/mapp_capstone/128, accessed on 21st September 2021.

[26] K.D. Neff, K.L. Kirkpatrick, and S.S. Rude (2007). 'Self-compassion and Adaptive Psychological Functioning'. *Journal of research in personality*, 41(1), pp. 139-154.

[27] V.A. Naushad, J.J. Bierens, K.P. Nishan, C.P. Firjeeth, O.H. Mohammad, A.M. Maliyakkal, and M.D. Schreiber (2019). 'A Systematic Review of the Impact of Disaster on the Mental Health of Medical Responders'. *Prehospital and disaster medicine*, 34(6), pp. 632–643.

[28] A.T. O'Donnell, F. Corrigan, and S. Gallagher (2015). 'The Impact of Anticipated Stigma on Psychological and Physical Health Problems in the Unemployed Group'. *Frontiers in psychology*, 6, 1263. http://dx.doi.org/10.3389/fpsyg.2015.01263, accessed on 12th May 2021

[29] T. Ramaci, M. Barattucci, C. Ledda, and V. Rapisarda (2020). 'Social Stigma during COVID-19 and its Impact on HCWs Outcomes'. *Sustainability*, 12(9), pp. 38–34. https://doi.org/10.3390/su12093834, accessed on 31st May 2021.

[30] R.P. Rajkumar (2020). 'COVID-19 and Mental Health: A Review of the Existing Literature'. *Asian journal of psychiatry*, 102066.

[31] A. Thamby and T.S. Jaisoorya (2020). 'Psychological Issues of Frontline Personnel Combating COVID-19'. *Mental Health in the times of COVID-19 Pandemic – Guidance for General Medical and Specialised Mental Healthcare Settings*. Department of Psychiatry, NIMHANS.

[32] D.K. Tracy, M. Tarn, R. Eldridge, J. Cooke, J.D. Calder, and N. Greenberg (2020). 'What should be Done to Support the Mental Health of Healthcare Staff Treating Covid-19 Patients?' *The British Journal of Psychiatry*, 217(4), 537–539.

[33] A. von Keudell, K.A. Koh, S.B. Shah, M.B. Harris, M. Smith, E.K. Rodriguez, and G. Dyer (2016). 'Mental Health After the Boston Marathon Bombing'. *The Lancet Psychiatry*, 3(9), pp. 802–804.

[34] R.Vaisya (2020). 'The Plight of Healthcare Workers in India during the COVID-19 Pandemic'. *The Pharma Times News Bureau*. Retrieved from http://thepharmatimes.in/the-plight-of-health-care-workers-in-india-during-covid-19-pandemic/, accessed on 7th July 2021.

[35] World Health Organisation (2020). WHO announces COVID-19 outbreak a pandemic. Retrieved from https://www.euro.who.int/en/health-topics/health-emergencies/coronavirus-covid-19/news/news/2020/3/who-announces-covid-19-outbreak-a-pandemic, accessed on 15th August 2021.

[36] World Health Organisation (2020). Coronavirus Disease (COVID-19). Retrieved from https://www.who.int/health-topics/coronavirus#tab=tab_1, accessed on 15th August 2021.

[37] World Health Organisation (2008). International Health Regulations (2005). Retrieved from https://www.who.int/publications/i/item/9789241580410, accessed on 26th July 2021.

[38] World Health Organisation (2020). Preventing violence against health workers. Retrieved from https://www.who.int/activities/preventing-violence-against-health-workers, accessed on 18th September 2021.

[39] J. Xing, N. Sun, J. Xu, S. Geng, and Y. Li, 2020. 'Study of the Mental Health Status of Medical Personnel Dealing with New Coronavirus Pneumonia'. *PLoS One*, 15(5), p.e 0233145.

[40] W.R. Zhang, K. Wang, L. Yin, W.F. Zhao, Q. Xue, M. Peng, and H. Chang, (2020). 'Mental Health and Psychosocial Problems of Medical Health Workers during the Covid-19 Epidemic in China'. *Psychotherapy and Psychosomatics*, pp. 1–9.

CHAPTER 4

Mental Health in Disaster Risk Reduction: An Evidence Based Review

A. Shahin Sultana[1]

Abstract: *In the recent decades, disasters have become a common occurrence in human lives. It is necessary to admit that disasters disrupt communities and cause widespread destruction, injury, and displacement (Evans et al., 2021) and it is vital to engage measures to deal with them efficiently. Developing countries are more prone to disasters and mental health issues caused by disasters are even more neglected (Makwana, 2019). Understanding the disaster risk reduction mechanism and strategies as well as learning how to strengthen them periodically is the only modality envisaged now. In this endeavour, it is necessary to examine and disseminate the data predominant in this field, understand the strengths and inadequacies of the existing literature in both local and global contexts, and improvise the developing knowledge in this regard accordingly. This paper shall engage in the narrative review method and document the existing knowledge with an emphasis on integrating mental healthcare in disaster risk reduction, its rationale and necessity, ways to deal with it to thwart more such calamities, and loss of human lives and resources.*

Keywords: Disasters, Mental Health, Disaster Risk Reduction, Disaster Mental Healthcare, Knowledge, Evidence Based Review

Introduction

The term 'disaster' originates from the French word desastre meaning 'des' 'aster', together referred to as 'bad or evil star' (TNAU, 2015). Disasters are an occurrence which cause severe disturbances to a community surpassing its ability to use their own assets and materials. However, there is no universal definition of disaster as it differs from one context to another. A disaster generally gets triggered either by natural,

[1] Professor, The Department of Social Work, The School of Social Sciences and International Studies, Pondicherry University, Pondicherry.
E-mail: shahin.samroh@gmail.com

man-made and technological hazards or due to numerous other factors that impact the exposure and helplessness of a community (IFRC, 2021).

Mizutori (2020) remarks "Disaster happens when a community is not appropriately resourced or organised to withstand the impact, and whose population is vulnerable because of poverty, exclusion or socially disadvantaged in some way." In this process, the concept of disaster risk management can be best understood as engaging policies and strategies of disaster risk reduction to ward off the forthcoming disasters, reduce the risks associated with the prevailing ones, minimise the losses during their occurrences, and build resilience among the stakeholders. These modalities can be referred to as prospective, corrective, compensatory and residual disaster management practices (UNDRR, 2020).

However, the field of disaster management has witnessed the shift in focus to disaster risk reduction as part of disaster risk management (Gray et al., 2020). Disaster risk reduction aims to prevent and minimise the impact caused by various disasters be it earthquakes, floods, droughts, and storms. It is certain that the advantages of financing disaster risk reduction influences the lives and well-being of individuals post and pre disaster processes. Therefore, it is imperative that their benefits are guaranteed (USAID, 2019). Ecosystem based Disaster Risk Reduction (Eco-DRR) is referred to as the sustainable management, conservation, and restoration of ecosystems with the objective of reducing the disasters at first and then subsequently developing sustainability and resilience in communities (IUCN, 2021).

At this juncture, there is a need for a fundamental shift in how risk is perceived, if resilience is to be achieved. The objective of resilience is not only to confront the disaster and its aftermath rather investing time and energy in building resilient individuals and communities. A shift in the mindset can be only achieved if a risk-informed investment (social, economic and environmental) happens as part of the norm and then the gains can be witnessed subsequently. It is vital that a radical transformation happens where the government and the private sector financing priorities and systems include, but not limited to, multi-lateral and bi-lateral aid funding where more investment is put at the prevention end of the cycle than the response end. This is the main thrust on which the UN office for disaster risk reduction is based with respect to the risk reduction strategies (Mizutori, 2019).

There is a growing need to understand that frequent occurrences of disasters hamper social and economic well-being and the only way which could be thought in this backdrop are modalities to prevent disasters at one end and enabling the processes engaged in relief, reconstruction, recovery, and rehabilitation of human lives and systems. On the other hand, if both do not go hand in hand there will be an anticipated loss in terms of human, financial, structural, and other losses. There is a visible shift in the understanding and operation of disasters as from disaster management it is gradually been referred to as disaster risk reduction strategies as part of the entire process. Their focus remains well-being and welfare of individuals and communities at stake.

Disaster Risk Reduction: An Overview

Disasters have become a common occurrence every now and then and it impacts the mental health and well-being of individuals, groups, families, and communities at large. It has now become an inevitable part of our lives and we are left with no alternative than living with fears and anxieties associated with them. The most appropriate intervention at this juncture is to understand more about disasters, their natures, occurrences, causes, impacts, interventions required, and how to implement and integrate them successfully. In addition to this, what is necessary is a gradual shift in terms of approach towards risk reduction than to indulge in the blame game and be contented with disaster management practices. Disaster risk reduction should be the pivotal focus henceforth to move forward.

With respect to natural and man-made disasters, a very shallow formulation has been done. Evidences suggest that flooding can be a result of both deforestation and climate change probably triggered by both natural and social factors (Martin, 2010).

Disaster prevention helps save substantial amounts of resources when compared to allowing the disasters happen, subsequently providing paybacks across many time scales (Shreve et al., 2014). It is not easy to prevent disasters as it is not a one-time action or a single act. It includes processes which cover how people think and behave such as attitudes, paradigms, values, and cultures (Kruger et al., 2015).

Preventing disasters does not mean only dissemination of information but it should positively and tangibly impact day to day life such as improved drinking water, shelter, choices, energy, resources, food, education, and livelihoods. Analysing the vulnerabilities and their causes, including them as part of primary and secondary school curricula, and emulating how health, safety, and lifestyle issues can be included as part of this process (Kelman, 2019).

The Sendai Framework for disaster risk reduction proposes rise in funding in the field of innovation and technology development. It is of the opinion that risks associated with disasters can be effectively managed through these initiatives. However, it is unable to establish this on the basis of scientific evidence. Three issues have been identified to overcome these barriers which are (1) networking, (2) coproduction of knowledge, and (3) stronger role played by academia (Izumi et al., 2019).

It is pertinent that disaster risk reduction processes are best understood and multi-disciplinary perspectives be engaged in the process to foresee visible changes. The development of strategies down the line is not that simple however, it is time to move on keeping the welfare of people in mind and initiate discussions, policy making deliberations, research, and field work practice on the same. There is a need for a paradigm shift in the disaster management approaches accommodating the disaster risk reduction practices to contain rising disasters in the long run. The involvement of multi-stakeholders is envisaged in education, capacity building, awareness and dissemination on the same which can create a vibrant and robust force in minimising the disasters through multi-pronged approaches. The civil society has also a major role to play as small steps at the individual, family, and community level can result in the reduction of the risks and the frequencies of the disasters in the long run. Specific schemes and programmes solely targeting disaster risk reduction mechanisms have to be taken to all platforms such as educational institutions, healthcare systems, private, public, and the unorganized sector and many more spaces to turn this into a reality. The developing countries can prevent the breakdown of social, economic, and psychological well-being of individuals and communities by adopting disaster risk reduction strategies and mechanisms thereby creating a visible space in preventing disasters and also confront climate change.

The need for disaster risk reduction for the increased use of innovation and new technology has never been greater and recognised so much. However, a tremendous gap is witnessed in the interface of science, technology, and policy making (Izumi et al., 2019).

For mitigating the risks of disasters, the convergence of science and technology is crucial as it can foster innovation (Lee et al., 2018). To make such disaster risk reduction strategies effective and useful, it is important that both innovative products and approaches are taken into account while working on them to develop further (Izumi et al., 2019). It is necessary to know that innovation provides useful tools to cope with hazards (Huh et al., 2018).

Bangladesh government is appreciated for its different efforts and significant progress as the reason for decrease in number of deaths can be attributed to its successful disaster risk reduction strategies. In the case of cyclone Sidr in 2007, successful evacuation of coastal residents was observed (Paul, 2009). During the cyclone Alia, it was noticed that different people had different kinds of behavioural pattern at varying time period of weather and warning conditions. Many factors influence their decision-making process helping them to select the destination of their choice for evacuation subsequently (Parvin et al., 2019).

It has been witnessed that most Bangladeshi women have the sole responsibility of safety and taking care of children, all household assets, and belongings. It was women who took time to prepare for themselves, children, livestock, elders at their homes, as well as important and valuable materials and assets. The women overall took around 1-2 hours as preparation time when it came to evacuation. If men took 99.2 minutes, women took 125.2 minutes as part of evacuation (Parvin et al., 2019). This shows the gender difference in responsibilities they take towards their families in times of disaster as well.

Similarly, the climate change vulnerability on individuals, families, groups, and communities is diverse and impacts them differently. Human mental health and well-being is a complex interplay between genetic, psychological, social, lifestyle factors, and environmental exposures (Filipova et al., 2020). It is evident that disasters and mental health in a way are related to each other and the effect might have a negative impact on the population affected by disasters. At this juncture, it is necessary to understand and integrate mental healthcare into disaster risk reduction approaches but prior to that it is pertinent to examine and understand the impact and vulnerability of individuals as part of various disasters from existing literature on the same.

Disaster Mental Health Care

Disasters demand global attention as it is now a complex problem and it has become an inevitable truth of our lives. It is witnessed that every year individuals and communities are being affected by disasters and this in turn disrupts their mental health and well-being. The economic and social development has been frequently interrupted by the occurrence of natural disasters. It is observed that the global climate change is a gradual and subtle process. It is likely to have the most negative effect on mental health and well-being, especially among the most vulnerable populations. It can significantly impact those with pre-existing serious illnesses even worse comparatively (Doherty et al., 2011). Post disaster effects have witnessed a spurt in critical influences on the victims with respect to their socio-economic and mental states (Makwana, 2019).

The developing countries will be more susceptible with respect to the occurrences of disasters as they possess critical challenges like poverty, resource shortages, educational constraints, and limited infrastructural challenges coupled with inadequate trained manpower, awareness, and knowledge with respect to mental health problems associated with disasters. Disasters happen so suddenly that the victims go into a state of shock, denial, and hopelessness. As a result, they experience anxiety and stress and are not able to come to terms with reality. The safest and most secure place for every individual and family is their home. When that gets affected, their lives are shattered. The impact on human mental health varies according to their losses such as that of loved ones, livelihood, assets, documents, cattle stock, properties, etc., and the time for recuperation from the same also varies accordingly depending on the mental strength and resilience of an individual (Peek, 2008).

Disasters and mental healthcare need serious discussions and deliberation. Individuals go through different kinds of experiences and they have impacted them differently. Some have lost their homes, some their dear and near ones, some livelihood, some their valuable assets, possessions and many more. It leaves an indelible impression and impact on their lives. Some are able to recuperate with their own resilience, some with appropriate interventions while some are not able to come out of those experiences. Hence, disasters impact individuals and communities differently.

Disasters negatively impact individuals socially and psychologically. However, government interventions limits itself largely to the social and financial aspects but there is a genuine developing demand for psychosocial interventions post disaster to retrieve the victims back thereby ensuring their wellness and well-being (Makwana, 2019).

Various studies have explained the physical and psychological health effects of floods (Tapsell, 2002). Jenkins and Meltzer (2012) document the post Indian Ocean tsunami (2004) impacts on the mental health status of the victims. Similarly, the survivors from the Nordic countries have also observed a rise in the incidence of mental health disturbances. Kar, N. (2010) states that people who have witnessed Mumbai riots in 1992-93 and those affected were left in fear, shock, and helplessness unable to cope with the experience they went through suddenly in their lives.

Disasters impacts individual, inter-group relations, social, and structural changes with a larger impact on their mental health and well-being (Galea, Nandi, and Vlahov, 2005). Natural disasters can trigger traumatic and acute illness. Similarly, Van den Berg, Grievink, Yzermans, and Lebret (2005) points out to somatic disorders as the result of disasters.

Marshall et al. (2007) reports critical forms of depression and Fritze et al. (2008) highlights problems like drug and alcohol abuse, high rates of suicide, and abuse as after effects of disasters. Vulnerability of the stakeholders, pre and post disaster, is a serious concern and it is quite intense with children, women, elderly, and the specially-abled.

Children experience Post Traumatic Stress Disorder (PTSD), depression, anxiety, emotional distress and sleep disorders due to their vulnerabilities and differences post disaster. Some of the common symptoms post disaster are severe and uncontrollable stress, feelings of grief and sadness for a longer duration, substance dependency, adjustment problems, etc., resulting in family conflicts (Makwana, 2019).

Kar, N. (2010) comments that post Mumbai riots the psychological and behavioural symptoms observed were suicide attempts, unnecessary fear, state of suspiciousness, paranoia, obsessed thoughts, and sexual inactivity. He further comments post bomb blasts in a bus in 1996 at Dausa, Rajasthan people reported severe stress, state of helplessness, severe mood swings, and forgetfulness.

The Bhopal gas tragedy was an eyeopener in understanding the mental health dimension of disasters where it was witnessed that those who were victims experienced psychopathological symptoms which affected them to a larger extent in their day-to-day lives (Murthy, 2014). In this regard, Kar, N. (2010) also added that most of the victims in this disaster were females, most of them also suffered from variety of mental disorders.

The extent to which the victims get affected mentally due to disasters is unimaginable and it impacts the society differently. The awareness level among public, at large, on the same is too minimal (Hossain et al., 2019). Climate change is most often seen as an environmental issue than a psychological one (Koger et al., 2011). It is necessary to establish it as a public health problem and advocate behavioural changes to confront the same in the near future (Rowe, 2002). Climate change affects social identity and personal well-being (Doherty et al., 2011).

Post disasters there is a surge in the psychological symptoms and other traumatic experiences. All these impacts the victims and their communities largely (Makwana, 2019) and some of them become irreversible inadvertently, without appropriate and timely interventions.

In India, mental health issues in general, has been a neglected subject as it is still considered as a stigmatised problem. With respect to disasters and mental health issues, they are further neglected (Makwana N., 2019). This is really worrisome as the subsequent effects post disaster can impact the individuals, families, and communities to a larger extent and if not attended to efficiently, it can have disastrous effects not only for the current generation but also future generations to come. Interventions help the victims to normalise mental health despite their losses. It has been witnessed that the victims who might have developed mental health symptoms with the help of psychoeducation, counselling, and other interventions are encouraged to lead a better and positive life. They turn out to be an asset in the task force and a resourceful contribution to their own communities. It is time to realise that disaster risk reduction should be taken seriously and propagated with full sincerity and acted upon to minimise the risks, incidents of disasters and indirectly minimise the mental health concerns and problems which otherwise might destabilise individuals and communities. Stabilising economy through hardships can be attained comparatively than reversing mental health problems and deformities of individuals as the vulnerabilities and the risks are higher. Similarly, financial implications shall also be higher if risks associated with disasters are not attended to timely. The focus should be to strengthen disaster risk reduction strategies. Mechanisms should be further rolled out to action with multi-disciplinary task force both at the government and non-governmental side including academicians, policy makers, civil society, health professionals such as social work professionals and psychologists. In this purview, the risks can be minimised and mental health concerns can be checked to a larger extent as it is the need of the hour.

Conclusion

The main purpose of this paper has been to understand the interconnect between disasters and mental health. In this regard, an attempt is made to examine the inter-relatedness based on existing literature. Through these, varied impacts have been identified. The need for pre and post disaster interventions has also evolved from the highlights of the reviews presented. Mental health is an integral part of disaster risk reduction interventions and this needs to be deliberated upon further and be strengthened to build resilient individuals, communities, and nations. Multidisciplinary perspectives can be encouraged for understanding rehabilitating the clients in need as part of disaster risk reduction strategies. There is a lot of scope for research and development in the process of integrating mental health as part of disaster risk reduction and government as well as other funding agencies can come forward to provide adequate funding on diverse themes related to these, as this is one of the most genuine and crucial emerging challenges in the field of disaster risk reduction.

Resilience does not mean just the ability to deal effectively with negative situations and get back to normalcy but preparing one for future situation and vulnerabilities on the same (Folke, 2002).

Zhang et al. (2013) identifies two level of psychological interventions: (a) the basic routine psychological interventions with psychological education, support, and relaxation techniques; (b) high level psychological interventions which worked with emotions, characteristics, economic change, and factors.

Disasters not only disrupt the quality of life of individuals and families but creates significant burden on mental health conditions of individuals and communities. Hence, appropriate pre and post disaster interventions have to be planned to attend to the varied mental health problems triggered as part of an event (Makwana, 2019). Resilience not only promotes physical, social, and emotional well-being but also acts as an important protective factor (Aiena, 2015). Supportive strategies including emotional and material strategies happen to be of great help to deal with post disaster experiences (Wachinger, 2013). Rehabilitation plans also need to be rolled out keeping in mind the cultural context of the affected population (Makwana, 2019).

Disaster risk reduction includes many disciplines like natural sciences, applied sciences, technology, health, etc., and includes relevant resources and skills of both scientific and technical nature (UNISDR,

2013 and Baaz et al., 2002). The Sendai Framework for Disaster Risk Reduction (SFDRR) has been very encouraging in terms of investment in developing innovation and technology in long-term problem-solving measures in disaster risk reduction to attend the shortcomings, inter-dependencies, societal challenges, and risks associated with the disasters (Izumi et al., 2019). It is expected that there shall be measures initiated at all fronts towards minimising the risks associated with the occurrence of disasters and commitment from every individual in making the world a better and safe place to live in, not only for the present but also for the future generations.

References

[1] B.J. Aiena, B.J. Baczwaski, S.E. Schulenberg, E.M. Buchanan (2015). 'Measuring Resilience with the RS–14: A Tale of Two Samples'. *Journal of Personality Assessment*, May 4; 97(3), pp. 291–300.

[2] A. Boaz, C. Hayden (2002). 'Pro-active Evaluators: Enabling Research to be Useful, Usable and Used'. *Evaluation* 8(4), pp. 440–53.

[3] T.J. Doherty, and S.D. Clayton (2011). 'The Psychological Impacts of Global Climate Change'. *American Psychologist*, 66, pp. 265–276. doi: 10.1037/a002314.

[4] C.M. Evans, R.M. Adams, and L. Peek (2021). 'Incorporating Mental Health Research into Disaster Risk Reduction: An Online Training Module for the Hazards and Disaster Workforce'. *Int. J. Environ. Res. Public Health 2021*, 18, 1244. https://doi.org/10.3390/ijerph18031244. Accessed on 24 August 2021.

[5] T. Filipova, L. Kopsieker, E. Gerritsen, E. Bodin, B. Brzezinski, and O. Rubio-Ramirez (2020). 'Mental Health and the Environment: How European Policies can Better Reflect Environmental Degradation's Impact on People's Mental Health and Well-Being'. *Background paper by the Institute for European Environmental Policy (IEEP) and the Barcelona Institute for Global Health (ISGlobal).*

[6] C. Folke (2002). 'Social-ecological Resilience and Behavioural Responses'. Beijer International Institute of Ecological Ecological Economics, Royal Swedish Academy of Sciences, Sweden.

[7] J.G. Fritze, G.A. Blashki, S. Burke, and J. Wiseman (2008). 'Hope, Despair and Transformation: Climate Change and the Promotion from Katrina'. *Disaster mental health service in the Gulf Coast region.*

[8] S. Galea, A. Nandi, and D. Vlahov (2005). 'The Epidemiology of Posttraumatic Stress Disorder after Disasters'. *Epidemiologic Reviews*, 27, pp. 78–91. doi:10.1093/epirev/mxi003

[9] B. Gray, F. Hanna, and L. Reifels (2020). 'The Integration of Mental Health and Psychosocial Support and Disaster Risk Reduction: A Mapping and

Review'. *Int. J. Environ. Res. Public Health 2020*, 17, 1900. https://doi.org/10.3390/ijerph17061900

[10] H.M. Mahbub and N. Purohit (2019). Improving Child and Adolescent Mental Health in India: Status, Services, Policies, and Way Forward. Retrieved from http://www.indianjpsychiatry.org/article.asp, accessed on 30 September, 2020.

[11] H. Hu, T. Lei, J. Hu, S. Zhang, and P. Kavan (2018). 'Disaster-Mitigating and General Innovative Responses to Climate Disasters: Evidence from Modern and Historical China'. *International Journal of Disaster Risk Reduction*, 28, pp. 664–73.

[12] IFRC (2021). What is a Disaster? The International Federation of Red Cross and Red Crescent Societies. Retrieved from https://www.ifrc.org/what-disaster, accessed on 24 October, 2021.

[13] IUCN (2021). 'Disaster Risk Reduction. Commission on Ecosystem Management'. Retrieved from https://www.iucn.org/commissions/commission-ecosystem-management/our-work/cems-thematic-groups/disaster-risk-reduction, accessed on 24 October, 2021.

[14] T. Izumi, R. Shaw, R. Djalante, M. Ishiwatari, and T. Komino (2019). 'Disaster Risk Reduction and Innovations'. *Progress in Disaster Science*, 2590-0617/© 2019. Elsevier. Retrieved from http://dx.doi.org/10.1016/j.pdisas.2019.100033

[15] R. Jenkins, and H. Meltzer (2012). 'The Mental Health Impacts of Disasters'. Government Office of Science, UK. 2012.

[16] R.D. Marshall, R.A. Bryant, L. Amsel, E.J. Suh, J.M. Cook, and Y. Neria (2007). 'The Psychology of Ongoing Threat: Relative Risk Appraisal, the September 11 Attacks, and Terrorism-Related Fears'. *American Psychologist*, 62, 304 –316. doi:10.1037/0003-066X.62.4.304

[17] N. Kar (2010). 'Indian Research on Disaster and Mental Health'. *Indian journal of psychiatry*. Jan; 52(Suppl 1):S286

[18] I. Kelman (2019). 'Axioms and Actions for Preventing Disasters'. *Progress in Disaster Science*. Elsevier. Retrieved from http://dx.doi.org/10.1016/j.pdisas.100008

[19] M. Koger Susan, E. Leslie Kerry, and D. Hayes Erica (2011). 'Climate Change: Psychological Solutions and Strategies for Change'. *Ecopsychology*. Mary and Leibert Incl. December. Vol. 3, No. 4, 227–235. DOI:10.1089/eco.2011.0041

[20] F. Krüger, G. Bankoff, T. Cannon, B. Orlowski, E.L. Schipper (2015). 'Cultures and Disasters: Understanding Cultural Framings in Disaster Risk Reduction'. F. Routledge, London and New York.

[21] C. Lee, G. Park, and J. Kang (2018). 'The Impact of Convergence between Science and Technology on Innovation'. *Journal of Technology Transfer 2018*; 43: 522–44.

[22] N. Makwana (2019). 'Disaster and Its Impact on Mental Health: A Narrative Review'. *J Family Med Prim Care*, 8: 3090-5.

[23] B.K. Marshall and J.S. Picou (2008). 'Postnormal Science, Precautionary May–June 2011'. *American Psychologist Professional Psychology*.

[24] M.L. Martin (2010). 'Child Participation in Disaster Risk Reduction: The Case of Flood-affected Children in Bangladesh'. *Third World Quarterly*. Dec 1, 2010; 31(8): 1357–75.

[25] M. Mizutori (2019). 'From Risk to Resilience: Pathways for Sustainable Development'. *Progress in Disaster Science*, Volume 2, July, Elsevier.

[26] M. Mizutori (2020). Time to Say Goodbye to Natural Disasters. Retrieved from https://www.preventionweb.net/blog/time-say-goodbye-natural-disasters, accessed on 20 October, 2021.

[27] R.S. Murthy (2014). 'Mental Health of Survivors of 1984 Bhopal Disaster: A Continuing Challenge'. *Industrial psychiatry journal*. Jul; 23(2): 86.

[28] G.A. Parvin, M. Sakamoto, R. Shaw, H. Nakagawa, and M.S. Sadik (2019). 'Evacuation Scenarios of Cyclone Aila in Bangladesh: Investigating the Factors Influencing Evacuation Decision and Destination'. *Progress in Disaster Science*, 2, [100032]. https://doi.org/10.1016/j.pdisas.2019.100032

[29] B.K. Paul (2009). Why Relatively Fewer People Died? The Case of Bangladesh's Cyclone, *Sidr. Nat Hazards*, 50(2): 289–304.

[30] L. Peek (2008). 'Children and Disasters: Understanding Vulnerability, Developing Capacities, and Promoting Resilience—An Introduction'. *Children Youth and Environments*. Jan 1; 18(1): 1–29.

[31] D. Rowe (2002). 'Environmental Literacy and Sustainability as Core Requirements: Success Stories and Models'. In W.L. Filho (Eds.), *Teaching sustainability at universities: Toward curriculum greening*. New York: Peter Lang International Academic Publishers.

[32] C.M. Shreve and I. Kelman (2014). 'Does Mitigation Save? Reviewing Cost-Benefit Analyses of Disaster Risk Reduction'. *Int J Disaster Risk Reduct*; 10(A), pp. 213–35.

[33] S.M. Tapsell, E.C. Penning Rowsell, S.M. Tunstall, and T.L. Wilson (2002). 'Vulnerability to Flooding: Health and Social Dimensions'. *Philosophical transactions of the royal society of London. Series A: Mathematical, Physical and Engineering Sciences*. May 24; 360 (1796): 1511 25.

[34] Tamil Nadu Agricultural University Agritech Portal (2015). Disaster Management. Tamil Nadu Agricultural University. Retrieved from https://agritech.tnau.ac.in/agriculture/agri_majorareas_disastermgt_anintroduction.html, accessed on 25 October, 2021.

[35] UNDRR (2020). Disaster Risk Management. United Nations Office for Disaster Risk Reduction. Retrieved from https://www.undrr.org/terminology/disaster-risk-management, accessed on 20 October, 2021.

[36] UNISDR (2013). Using Science for Disaster Risk Reduction: Report of the UNISDR Scientific and Technical Advisory Group 2013.

[37] USAID (2019). Disaster Risk Reduction. Usaid from the American People. Retrieved from https://www.usaid.gov/what-we-do/working-crises-and-conflict/disaster-risk-reduction, accessed on 25 October, 2021.

[38] B. Van den Berg, L. Grievink, J. Yzermans, and E. Lebret (2005). 'Medically Unexplained Physical Symptoms in the Aftermath of Disasters'. *Epidemiologic Reviews*, 27, pp. 92–106. doi: 10.1093/epirev/mxi001

[39] G. Wachinger, O. Renn, C. Begg, and C. Kuhlicke (2013). 'The Risk Perception Paradox—Implications for Governance and Communication of Natural Hazards'. *Risk analysis*. Jun; 33(6): 1049–65.

[40] N. Zhang, H. Hong, X. Jihong, and L. Yuntao (2013). 'Research on Post-Disaster Psychological Intervention and Reconstruction Model'. In *IEEE Conference Anthology*. 2013 Jan 1; 1–4.

CHAPTER 5

Awareness on Child Inclusive Disaster Risk Management Among the Stakeholders

Santosh Kumar[1] **and Balu I.**[2]

Abstract: *This study was commissioned to analyse the awareness on child centric disaster risk reduction (CCDRR) among stakeholders in India. Multi-stage sampling method was used in this study. This study was conducted in Kerala, Odisha, Maharashtra, Punjab, and Tripura covering 300 respondents. The study found that only one-fourths of the stakeholders have good and poor awareness, respectively. Awareness on child centric disaster risk reduction in the country is not satisfactory. Female stakeholders having better awareness than male stakeholders. Civil society organisations have better awareness than government officers. Stakeholders from women and child welfare and revenue department have better awareness than other departments. It was found that there is a strong association between states, departments, and awareness.*

Keywords: Awareness, Child Centric, Knowledge, and Stakeholders

Introduction

Children are physically vulnerable to both man-made and natural disaster events due to their dependency on adults. However, the abilities and creativity of older children and adolescents are an asset in disaster risk management. Disasters not only disrupt children's routine life but they may also result in missing school days and slow academic progress, reduced social opportunities, and exacerbating exposure to various life stressors. It is essential to focus on the protection of children by adopting effective risk mitigation measures.

[1] Professor & Head, Governance, Public Policy and Inclusive Disaster Risk Reduction, National Institute of Disaster Management, Delhi.
E-mail: profsantosh@gmail.com

[2] Child Centric Disaster Risk Reduction Centre, National Institute of Disaster Management, Delhi. E-mail: baluinidm@gmail.com

Children in hazard-prone areas in our country are twice as likely to be living in chronic poverty and thrice as likely to become impoverished according to a major new study by the Overseas Development Institute (ODI). Children's experience of climate and natural hazard-related disasters vary depending on the context in which they are living with the poorest of poor being very likely to be affected. Disasters and climate hazards are affecting children and adolescents in multiple ways, directly through injury or impact on poverty or individual deprivation and indirectly through the implications on essential services and systems central to the well-being and long-term development of children.

Review of Literature

Disasters have an uneven impact on the poor in developing countries, especially affecting the most vulnerable sections of the population. Young children, especially differently abled children, are less well equipped to deal with deprivation and stress due to their particular physical and psychosocial character (Bartlett, 2008; Cutter, 1995 and Peek, 2008). These leaves children particularly vulnerable to the effects of disasters. In the late 1990s, the number of children affected by disasters was huge (estimated at 66.5 million per year). The impact of climate change is projected to increase this to as many as 175 million per year in the forthcoming decade.

'Children constitute an extremely huge percentage of those who are most vulnerable and the effects, especially for the youngest children, can be long term. If speculations about the impacts of climate change on children fail to take into account the particular vulnerabilities and capacities of children at different ages, gender, ability measures for prevention, mitigation, and adaptation, it may prove to be insufficient in critical ways and may even result in additional stresses for young children' (Bartlett, 2008). Foster (1995) stated that children from landless households in disaster affected areas experienced a significant deterioration of their health and nutritional status, which the author attributes in part to credit market imperfections.

The incidence of child malnutrition also increased more than three times among households that are more exposed to heavy rainfall during the hurricane Mitch in Nicaragua in late 1998 (Baez and Santos, 2007). In connection with this to reduce the disaster risk on children, awareness among the stakeholders on child centric disaster risk reduction is essential. Since child centric disaster risk reduction is a new concept, much literature about awareness on child centric disaster risk reduction is not available.

Materials and Methods

This study was conducted to find the level of awareness about child centric disaster risk reduction among the stakeholders in India. Multi-stage sampling method was used in this study and one sate from each region was selected. From the selected states, sixty respondents were chosen from a population of trainees who participated in training programmes on child centric disaster risk reduction by adopting simple random sampling method. The survey was conducted before the training programme began. The respondents were from the department of health, education, revenue, women and child welfare, panchayat raj, and rural development first responders and civil society. Total sample size of 300 was achieved by adopting simple random sampling method (Table 1).

Table 1: Sampling States

Region	*Name of the State*	*No. of Respondents*
South	Kerala	60
West	Maharashtra	60
East	Odisha	60
North	Punjab	60
North East	Tripura	60
Total	5	300

Source: Primary data collected from field.

To analyse the data, Statical Package for Social Science has been used. Also chi-square test using SPSS was used to find the association of selected independent variables with awareness among the stakeholders on child centric disaster risk reduction

Findings

This study has covered awareness on basic concepts of disaster, child rights and disaster risk reduction, disaster impact on children, reducing vulnerabilities and enhancing capacity of children, and child centric disaster risk reduction.

Awareness on Basic Concepts of Disaster Management

It is evident from Table 2 that Kerala (53 per cent) and Odisha (50 per cent) are the top two states having good awareness on basic concepts of disaster management. On the other hand, Tripura (38 per cent) and Maharashtra (15 per cent) are the bottom two states having good awareness on basic concepts of disaster management. Maharashtra (47 per cent) and Odisha (23 per cent) are the top two states having poor awareness on basic concept of disaster management followed by Kerala (12 per cent) and Punjab (10 per cent) which are the bottom two states having poor awareness on basic concepts of disaster management. Overall, more than one third (40 per cent) of the stakeholders have good awareness on basic concepts of disaster management. A similar type of study was conducted among the college students in Kashmir valley and it was found that more than two-thirds of students know what disaster preparedness means (Bilal, Sidra-Ul-Mutahi, and Anees, 2017). The study also revealed about awareness on disaster plan and mock drill. Comparatively, the students have good awareness than government officers.

Table 2: Awareness on Basic Concepts of Disaster Management

States	*Poor*	*Average*	*Good*	*Total*
Kerala	7	21	32	60
	12.0%	35.0%	53.0%	100.0%
Maharashtra	28	23	9	60
	47.0%	38.0%	15.0%	100.0%
Odisha	14	16	30	60
	23.0%	27.0%	50.0%	100.0%
Punjab	6	28	26	60
	10.0%	47.0%	43.0%	100.0%
Tripura	12	25	23	60
	20.0%	42.0%	38.0%	100.0%
Total	67	113	120	300
	22.0%	38.0%	40.0%	100.0%

Source: Primary data collected from field.

Awareness on Child Rights and Disaster Risk Reduction

It is apparent from Graph 1 that Punjab (24 per cent) and Odisha (14 per cent) are the top two states having good awareness on child rights and disaster risk reduction. On the other hand, Maharashtra (12 per cent) and Tripura (10 per cent) are the bottom two states having good awareness. Tripura (68 per cent) and Maharashtra (65 per cent) are the top two states having poor awareness while Kerala (50 per cent) and Punjab (43 per cent) are the bottom two states having poor awareness. Overall, only 14 per cent of the stakeholders have good awareness and more than half (56 per cent) of the stakeholders are having poor awareness on child rights and disaster risk reduction of children.

Syed Mohsin Raja and Dhriti Sundar Gupta (2014) stated in their study that majority of (nearly 9 out of 10) respondents were aware of right to education. They also found that only less than half of the respondents were aware of right to participation. More than half of the respondents were aware of right to protection, right to development, and right to survival. The present study found that more than half of the respondents have poor awareness about rights of the children.

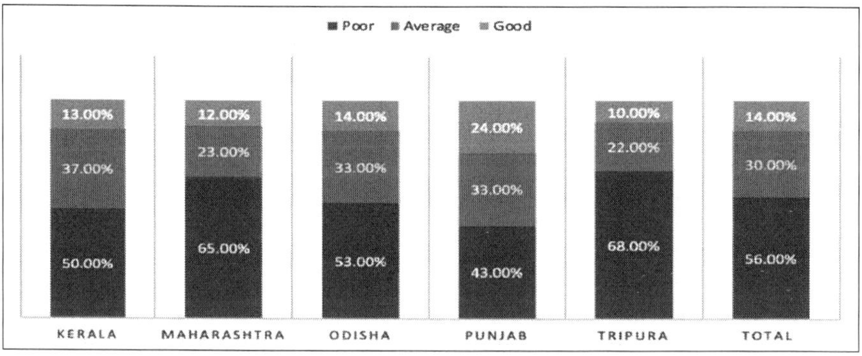

Graph 1: Awareness on Child Rights and Disaster Risk Reduction

Awareness about Disaster Impact on Children

Table 3 shows that Kerala (32 per cent) and Maharashtra (10 per cent) are the top two sates having good awareness about disaster impacts on children. On the other hand, Tripura (5 per cent) and Punjab (3 per cent) are the bottom two states having good awareness about disaster impacts on children. Punjab (80 per cent) and Odisha (55 per cent) are the top two state having poor awareness about disaster impact on children while Maharashtra (40 per cent) and Kerala (35 per cent) are the bottom two states having poor awareness about disaster impacts on children. Overall, only 11 per cent of the stakeholders have good awareness about disaster impacts on children whereas more than half (52 per cent) of the stakeholders have poor awareness about disaster impacts on children.

Not much studies have been conducted on awareness about disaster impacts on children. A study on affected parents' and other stakeholders' perception of a fire disaster management in India (a situational analysis) was conducted by Sujata Satapathy and Ajinder Walia in 2007.

Table 3: Awareness about Disaster Impact on Children

States	*Poor*	*Average*	*Good*	*Total*
Kerala	21	20	19	60
	35.0%	33.0%	32.0%	100.0%
Maharashtra	24	30	6	60
	40.0%	50.0%	10.0%	100.0%
Odisha	33	23	4	60
	55.0%	38.0%	7.0%	100.0%
Punjab	48	10	2	60
	80.0%	17.0%	3.0%	100.0%
Tripura	30	27	3	60
	50.0%	45.0%	5.0%	100.0%
Total	156	110	34	300
	52.0%	37.0%	11.0%	100.0%

Source: Primary data collected from field.

Awareness about Vulnerability and Capacity of Children

It is evident from Graph 2 that Odisha (38 per cent) and Tripura (20 per cent) are the top two states having good awareness about vulnerability and capacity of children. On the other hand, Maharashtra (18 per cent) and Kerala (17 per cent) are the bottom two states having good awareness about vulnerability and capacity of children. Odisha (50 per cent) and Kerala (38 per cent) are the top two states having poor awareness about vulnerability and capacity of children while Maharashtra (37 per cent),

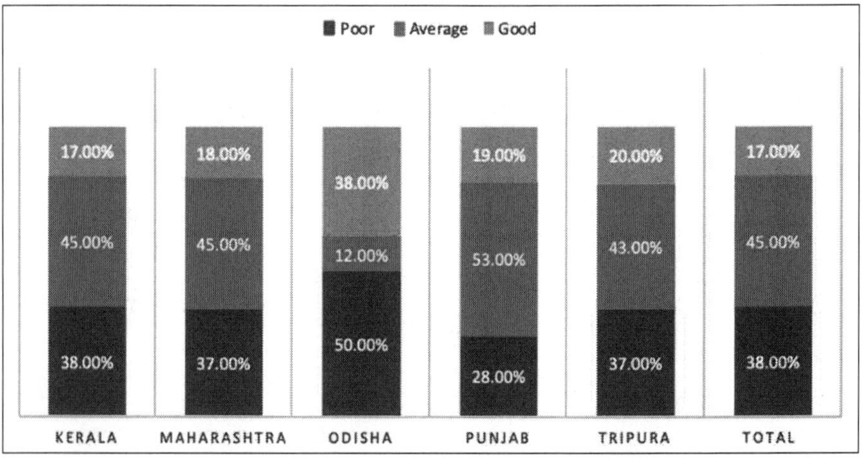

Graph 2: Awareness about Vulnerability and Capacity of Children

Source: Primary data collected from field.

Tripura (37 per cent), and Punjab (28 per cent) are the bottom three states having poor awareness about vulnerability and capacity of children. Overall, only 17 per cent of the stakeholders have good awareness about vulnerability and capacity of children.

More than one-thirds (38 per cent) of the stakeholders have poor awareness about vulnerability and capacity of children.

There is limited evidence on how hazard vulnerability capacity analysis tools help disaster managers to consider and address the risks and vulnerabilities. These are more prominent in urban contexts (Wigg, Maclure, Masson, V., and Gliozzo, 2018). The tools discussed in this study can help the stakeholders to gain knowledge on vulnerability and capacity of children.

Awareness about Child Centric Disaster Risk Reduction

It is apparent from Table 4 that Odisha (15 per cent) and Punjab (15 per cent) are the top two states having good awareness about child centric disaster risk reduction. On the other hand, Kerala (3 per cent) and Maharashtra (2 per cent) are the bottom two states having good awareness about child centric disaster risk reduction. Odisha (83 per cent) and Kerala (80 per cent) are the top two states having poor awareness about child centric disaster risk reduction while Tripura (63 per cent) and Punjab (40 per cent) are the bottom two states having poor awareness about child centric disaster risk reduction. Overall, only seven per cent of the stakeholders have good awareness about child centric disaster risk reduction. More

Table 4: Awareness about Child Centric Disaster Risk Reduction

States	*Poor*	*Average*	*Good*	*Total*
Kerala	48	10	2	60
	80.0%	17.0%	3.0%	100.0%
Maharashtra	44	15	1	60
	73.0%	25.0%	2.0%	100.0%
Odisha	50	1	9	60
	83.0%	2.0%	15.0%	100.0%
Punjab	24	27	9	60
	40.0%	45.0%	15.0%	100.0%
Tripura	38	19	3	60
	63.0%	32.0%	5.0%	100.0%
Total	204	72	24	300
	69.0%	24.0%	7.0%	100.0%

Source: Primary data collected from field.

than two-thirds (69 per cent) of the stakeholders have poor awareness about child centric disaster risk reduction.

Awareness about Child Centric Disaster Risk Reduction

It is evident from Table 5 that Punjab (12 per cent) and Kerala (4 per cent) are the top two states having excellent awareness about child centric disaster risk reduction. On the other hand, Odisha (0 per cent) and Maharashtra (0 per cent) are the bottom two states having excellent awareness about child centric disaster risk reduction. Punjab (28 per cent), Kerala (28 per cent), and Odisha (23 per cent) are the top three states having good awareness about child centric disaster risk reduction while Punjab (0 per cent) and Kerala (2 per cent) are the top two states having very poor awareness about child centric disaster risk reduction.

Table 5: Awareness about Child Centric Disaster Risk Reduction

States	*Very Poor*	*Poor*	*Fair*	*Good*	*Excellent*	*Total*
Kerala	1	11	29	17	2	60
	2.0%	18.0%	48.0%	28.0%	4.0%	100.0%
Maharashtra	4	18	30	8	0	60
	7.0%	30.0%	50.0%	13.0%	0.0%	100.0%
Odisha	7	19	20	14	0	60
	12.0%	32.0%	33.0%	23.0%	0.0%	100.0%
Punjab	0	3	33	17	7	60
	0.0%	5.0%	55.0%	28.0%	12.0%	100.0%
Tripura	4	12	31	11	2	60
	7.0%	20.0%	58.0%	18.0%	3.0%	100.0%
Total	16	63	143	67	11	300
	5.0%	21.0%	48.0%	22.0%	4.0%	100.0%

Source: Primary data collected from field.

It is revealed in Graph 3 that only 3 per cent of the stakeholders have excellent awareness about child centric disaster risk reduction followed by 22 per cent of the stakeholders with good awareness. The study found that only one-fourths of the stakeholders have good awareness and another one-fourth of the stakeholders have poor awareness. Nearly half (49 per cent) of the stakeholders have fair awareness about child centric disaster risk reduction. Overall,the awareness about child centric disaster risk reduction in the country is not favourable.

In most disasters, around a third or half of the deaths are that of children. Disasters affect children more disproportionally than adults, especially those from impoverished backgrounds in the long term (Kousky, 2016). Vulnerability of children is expected to increase as the intensity and frequency of natural disasters rise but the level of awareness about child centric disaster risk reduction among the stakeholders is not satisfactory and need national level concentration.

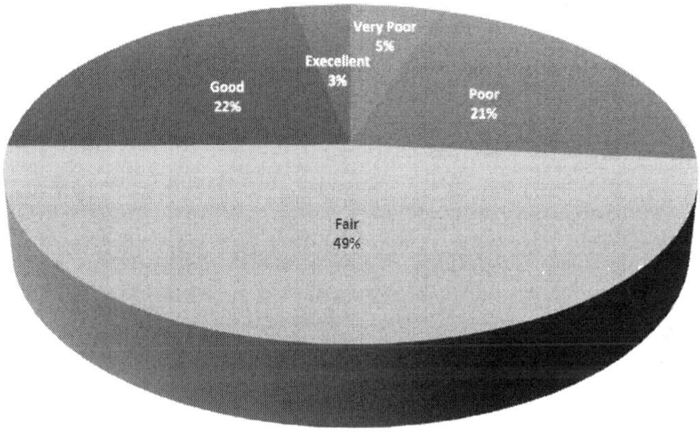

Graph 3: Awareness about Child Centric Disaster Risk Reduction

Source: Primary data collected from field.

Gender-wise Awareness

As shown in Table 6, 7 per cent of females are having excellent awareness while only 2 per cent of the males are having excellent awareness about child centric disaster risk reduction. About 30 per cent of the female stakeholders are having good awareness while only 24 per cent of the male stakeholders are having good awareness. Poor and very poor awareness among the male and female respondents are almost equal. Overall, female stakeholders have better awareness than the male stakeholders. Since children are much attached to a female so it is a positive finding that females have good awareness than the male stakeholders.

Table 6: Gender-wise Awareness

Gender	*Very Poor*	*Poor*	*Fair*	*Good*	*Excellent*	*Total*
Female	5	20	46	24	7	102
	5.0%	20.0%	45.0%	23.0%	7.0%	100.0%
Male	11	43	97	43	4	198
	5.0%	22.0%	49.0%	22.0%	2.0%	100.0%
Total	16	63	143	67	11	300
	5.0%	21.0%	48.0%	22.0%	4.0%	100.0%

Source: Primary data collected from field.

Department-wise Awareness

Graph 4 evidently depicts that civil society (10 per cent),women and child welfare (6 per cent), and revenue (6 per cent) departments are the top three departments having excellent knowledge about child centric disaster risk reduction. On the other hand, health (0 per cent), panchayat and rural development (0 per cent), and education (1 per cent) are the bottom three departments having excellent awareness about child centric disaster risk reduction. Civil society (19 per cent) health (9 per cent), and education (7 per cent) are the top three departments having very poor awareness about child centric disaster risk reduction while panchayat and rural development (0 per cent), first responders (0 per cent), and women and child welfare (2 per cent) are the bottom three departments having very poor awareness about child centric disaster risk reduction. Overall, awareness among the stakeholder of different departments is not appreciable.

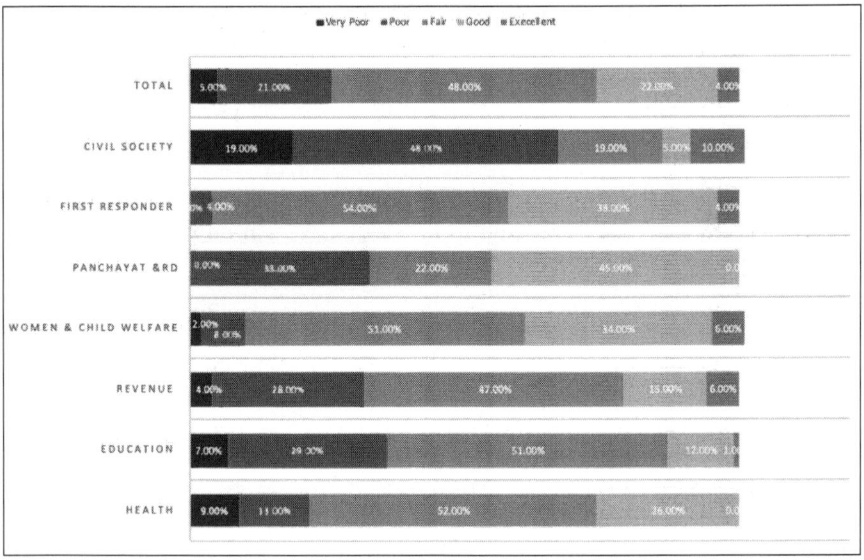

Graph 4: Department-wise Awareness

Source: Primary data collected from field.

Age-wise Awareness

Table 7 is evident that 8 per cent of below 30 years old stakeholders are having excellent awareness. Majority (29 per cent) of 30–40 years old stakeholders are having good awareness. Poor awareness found among more than one fourth of 41–50 years old and above 51 years old stakeholders. More than half of the below 30 years old (50 per cent), 30–40 years old (53 per cent), above 51 years old (52 per cent) having fair awareness on CCDRR. Study found that young stakeholders are having good awareness than old age stakeholders.

Table 7: Age-wise Awareness

Age Classification	*Very Poor*	*Poor*	*Fair*	*Good*	*Excellent*	*Total*
< 30	4	8	32	14	6	64
	6.0%	12.0%	50.0%	22.0%	8.0%	100.0%
30–40	2	8	31	17	1	59
	3.0%	14.0%	53.0%	29.0%	1.0%	100.0%
41–50	8	26	37	22	2	95
	9.0%	27.0%	39.0%	23.0%	2.0%	100.0%
> 51	2	21	43	14	2	82
	2.0%	26.0%	52.0%	17.0%	3.0%	100.0%
Total	16	63	143	67	11	300
	5.0%	21.0%	48.0%	22.0%	4.0%	100.0%

Source: Primary data collected from field.

Association of Selected Independent Variables with Awareness

States

Table 8 reveals that the calculated chi square value (45.751) is higher than the tabulated value leading to the null hypothesis (there is no association between states and awareness about child centric disaster risk reduction) being rejected. It means that there is a significant association between states and awareness about child centric disaster risk reduction.

Gender

According to Table 8, the calculated value of chi square value (4.815) is lesser than the tabulated value leading to the null hypothesis (there is no association between gender and awareness about child centric disaster risk reduction) being accepted. It means that there is no significant association between gender and awareness about child centric disaster risk reduction.

Department

Table 8 reveals that the calculated chi square value (68.049) is higher than the tabulated value leading to the null hypothesis (there is no association between department and awareness about child centric disaster risk reduction) being rejected. It means that there is a significant association between department and awareness about child centric disaster risk reduction.

Age

According to Table 8, the calculated value of chi square value (21.643) is lesser than the tabulated value leading to the null hypothesis (there is no association between age and awareness about child centric disaster risk reduction) being accepted. It means that there is no significant association between age and awareness about child centric disaster risk reduction.

Table 8: Association of Selected Independent Variables with Awarencss among the Stakeholders on Child Centric Disaster Risk Reduction

S. No.	*Independent Variables*	*Chi-square* (χ^2)
1	States	45.751**
2	Gender	4.815
3	Department	68.049**
4	Age	21.643

** Correlation is significant at the 0.01 level of probability
* Correlation is significant at the 0.05 level of probability
Source: Statistical package for social science (SPSS) software.

Conclusion

The present study found that only one-fourths of the stakeholders have good awareness and another one-fourth of the stakeholders have poor awareness. Nearly half of the stakeholders have fair awareness about child centric disaster risk reduction. Overall,the awareness about fourth child centric disaster risk reduction in the country is not favourable. Female stakeholders have better awareness than the male stakeholders. It was also observed that civil society has good awareness than the government officers. Stakeholders from the women and child welfare and revenue departments have better knowledge than other departments. The study also found that there is a significant association between states, departments, and awareness.

Odisha is the state which is the most vulnerable to disasters and has taken various steps for risk reduction of children indicating good knowledge. Similarly, Punjab and Kerala are highly educated states and have good awareness. Awareness is a part of preparedness for disaster risk reduction but present status of awareness on child centric disaster risk reduction. Among the stakeholders needs to be improved for the purpose of disaster risk reduction of children.

The National Disaster Management Authority (NDMA), National Institute of Disaster Management (NIDM), and Administrative Training Institutes should focus more on conducting training programmes for child centric disaster risk reduction of the stakeholders to improve their awareness thereby helping to reduce the vulnerability of children. The ministry of health, education, revenue, women and child welfare, panchayat raj and rural development should ensure that all their officers are attending the training programme on child centric disaster risk reduction.

Acknowledgement

This study was conducted with the participants of the training programme on child centric disaster risk reduction organised by the National Institute of Disaster Management and supported by United Nations International Children's Emergency Fund (UNICEF). I extend my gratitude to Major General Manoj Kumar Bindal, Prof. Santosh Kumar and Dr. Raka for their support and valuable guidance.

References

[1] S. Bartlett (2008). 'Climate Change and Urban Children – Impacts and Implications for Adaptation in Low- and Middle-Income Countries'. Human Settlements Discussion Paper.

[2] J. Baez and I. Santos (2007). Children's Vulnerability to Weather Shocks: A Natural Disaster as a Natural Experiment. Mimeo.

[3] B.A. Bhat, and S. Anees (2017). 'A Study on Disaster Awareness and Preparedness Among College Students In District Ganderbal of Kashmir Valley', *IJSART* – Volume 3, Issue 12, ISSN [ONLINE]: 2395–1052.

[4] S.L. Cutter (1995). The Forgotten Casualties: Women, Children, and Environmental Change. Global Environmental Change. 5.3: pp. 181–94.

[5] C. Kousky (2016). *Impacts of Natural Disasters on Children*, Vol. 26, Issue 1. Retrieved from www.futureofchildren.org.

[6] L. Peek (2008). Children and Disasters: Understanding Vulnerability, Developing Capacities and Promoting Resilience – An Introduction. Children, *Youth and Environments*, Vol. 18, pp. 1–29.

[7] S.M. Raja and D.S. Gupta (2014). Role of Social Media in Facilitating Awareness of Child Rights, Conference. National Seminar on Social Media and Democratic Discourse At: EFLU, Shillong

[8] S. Satapathy and A. Walia (2007). Affected Parents' and Other Stakeholders' Perception of a Fire Disaster Management in India: A Situational Analysis. Disaster Management & Response.

[9] J. Twigg, M. Maclure, V. Le Masson and G. Gliozzo (2018). Child-centred Hazard, Vulnerability and Capacity Assessment and Planning in Urban Settings: A Scoping Study and Needs Assessment. Research Report, Save the Children.

CHAPTER 6

COVID-19 Pandemic and Post Disaster Impact: A Study on Construction Workers in Tirupattur District

A. Xavier Susairaj[1], A. Premkumar[2] and A. Salaijayamani[3]

Abstract: *The present study is about the wage loss of the construction workers of Tirupattur in Tamil Nadu. Primary data was collected from 150 construction workers on the basis of random sampling during the pandemic period. The collected data were analysed with the help logistic regression analysis to identify the factors influencing wage loss of construction workers during the COVID-19 pandemic. The results of the study indicate a positive relationship between wage loss and COVID-19 pandemic. Further, the study also provides policy measures to overcome wage loss.*

Keywords: COVID, Pandemic, Construction Workers

Introduction

The SARS–CoV2 virus is the origin of COVID-19 (Abraham, 2020). One school of thought is that the coronavirus might have emerged through a natural spillover event. A bat coronavirus jumped species and infected humans either directly or through intermediary animals that in turn passed it to humans. New viral infection diseases, whether it is Human Immunodeficiency Virus/Acquired Immunodeficiency Syndrome, Ebola, Middle East Respirator Syndrome (MERS) or Nipah, have all arisen from spillover of animal virus to humans (Gauttam et al., 2021). The pandemic reflects (fundamental ecological equilibrium evidence has accumulated)

---

[1] Associate Professor and Head, Department of Economics, Sacred Heart College (Autonomous), Tirupattur, Tamil Nadu. E-mail: xsusairaj@shctpt.edu

[2] Research Scholar, Department of Economics, Sacred Heart College (Autonomous), Tirupattur, Tamil Nadu.

[3] Research Scholar, Department of Economics, Sacred Heart College (Autonomous), Tirupattur, Tamil Nadu.

that loss of biodiversity and ever increasing human incursions into the natural world have contributed heavily to the outbreak and spread of epidemic diseases.

The COVID-19 pandemic has severely disturbed economic activities. The global gross domestic product (GDP) has shrunk by 3 per cent in 2020 (IMF, 2020). During the first wave, we lost one lakh people in the world. During the second wave, more than 3.50 lakh lives were lost in this period alone. About 88 per cent of all the deaths comprised of people in the age group of 45 years and above, often sole bread winners of their families .A World Health Organization survey has found that 155 countries were the most affected ones by COVID-19.

During the second wave, unemployment rate was 8 per cent and the Indian economy had gone down to 7.3 per cent on April 2021 with 23 crore people living below the poverty line in India. It can be said that official records do not present the full picture of the pandemic deaths. In a country with too many socio-cultural factors inhabiting, recording of deaths and getting actual number of corona mortality cases becomes an improbability. The rural areas, largely, get omitted from the official counts. There was wide variation in testing across states and over time gender-wise COVID-19 has bitten men harder than women in India. The International Labour Organization survey reveals that 17 per cent of young people are likely to suffer from anxiety and depression. Child marriage has increased, abuse, trafficking and violence at home also increased due to COVID-19. The rural urban unemployment was high and migration of workers in urban areas have increased. Informal workers in India are referred to as unorganized workers. NCEUS (2006) estimates that in 2020 the total employment was in the category of formal employment (around 93 per cent).

Tamil Nadu COVID-19

Tamil Nadu state crossed 7 lakh COVID cases and it ranks fourth in terms of cases and it ranks second in terms of deaths, i.e. 9.05 per cent. The rapid antigen tests as well RT-PCR increased to 50,499 lakh tested people (Government of Tamil Nadu, 2021). Nearly, 25, 01,375 lakh people were discharged from hospitals in 2021. In this context, the present study analyses the impact of COVID-19 among the construction workers in Tirupattur district.

Problem of the Study

Some of the major problems regarding COVID-19 have been discussed here. The first issue is vaccine inequality, that is, mismatch between supply and demand. On the supply side, most of the vaccination centres are in urban areas. There is low uptake of vaccine among slum dwellers, rural people, and construction workers. Moreover, there is oxygen shortage in government hospitals. Many studies have shown that people were afraid of vaccine and hesitation regarding vaccination was also observed among people. Adequate cold chain infrastructure was not available in India. The underdeveloped countries were unable to provide masks or ventilators. The pandemic has also led to spike in the price of vegetables and other commodities. Due to lockdown, transportation has severely disrupted economic activity. Indian Council of Medical Research (ICMR) had estimated the prevalence of COVID-19 anti-bodies was lowest (68 per cent) in the country (Selvaraju et al., 2021).

It is to be noted that the delta variant was the primary reason for the majority of cases during the second wave in the rest of India, has been recently detected. Indian public health institution was unable to meet the challenges of any pandemic. Announced with a four hours' notice on 24 March 2020, the harsh unplanned national lockdown had created a house arrest scenario for a population of 1.2 billion in India. This triggered a crisis for the massive section of the urban workforce, who are mostly informally employed. This shut down sent cascading effects throughout manufacturing logistic, services, and construction workers. Barbara Harris-White (2007) observed that in low- and middle-income countries, very large proportions of construction workers were unemployed. Following are some important issues raised in the present study: number of days the construction workers had lost their wages and its effect on their family expenditure. In order to address these issues, the following are specific objectives of the present study:

1. To find out the reasons for wage loss of the construction workers due to COVID-19 in Tirupattur district.
2. To examine the socio-economic conditions of the construction workers.

Review of Literature

A systematic review has been conducted on the existing literature about COVID-19 impacts and construction workers in India. Google scholar database can be considered as the major source for collecting literature. Some of the studies found are as follows:

Celeste (2020) conducted a study on the experience of construction workers during COVID-19. The objective of the study was to identify the experience and feelings of construction workers during lockdown. The study found that construction workers faced an unexpected financial crisis, including rural and urban construction workers, during this pandemic. It has to be noted that age is one of the important factors among construction workers in terms of their health.

Soumi Majumder (2021) conducted a study on the impact of COVID-19 on the construction industry. The purpose of the study was to find out the problems faced in labour market, supply of material, company liquidity, and cost components. It was found that employers have some obligations on the health and safety of their employees such as prevention of occupational risk, provide necessary training, and monitoring the employees. The study suggests to provide good health and safety measures to the construction workers.

Makram et al. (2021) examined COVID-19 concerns raised by the construction workforce and development of mitigation practices. The objective of the study was to analyse construction related complaints submitted to the Occupational Safety and Health Administration complaint tracker and outline a list of recommendations to tackle those concerns. The study found that most of the construction workers were concerned about people who tested positive and were reported to work. Moreover, employees were not forced to wear mask during work hours on the construction site. The study suggested to monitor the employees during this pandemic situation for the safety of other construction workers.

Methods and Materials

Due to a smaller number of industries in Tirupattur district, most of the people are engage d in construction work as it is the major occupation of people living in and around Tirupattur. Therefore, Tirupattur district was selected as the study area. A structured interview schedule was employed to collect primary information on lockdown and its impacts from 150 construction workers in Tirupattur district on the basis of random sampling method. The study was conducted during the first nation-wide lockdown from April to June in 2020. The collected data was analysed with the support of Stata 11 software. The analysis part divided into four categories such as socio-economic characteristics, lockdown and its impact on construction workers, households monthly expenditure on various items, and association between wage loss and socio-economic characteristics. Chi-square test was employed to assess the relationship between wage and socio-economic factors of construction workers. Chi-square distribution was encountered during the collections of values that involve adding up squares. Variances of samples require adding a collection of squared quantities thus having distributions that are related to chi-square distribution (Gujarati, 2017).

Ethical Clearance

The work was completed with the approval from the Research Ethics Committee (REC) of Sacred Heart College (Autonomous), Tirupattur.

Analysis and Interpretation

Table 1 shows the socio-economic characteristics of the respondents. It reveals that majority of a smaller the respondents are males (67.3 per cent) and only 32.7 per cent of the respondents are females. In the age category, the majority of the respondents (20.7 per cent) are in the age group of 26 to 30 years followed by 20 per cent of the respondents in the age group of 36 to 40 years. Only 2.7 per cent of the respondents were less than 25 years old. In case of family size, majority of the households (22.7 per cent) had a family size of 6 members followed by 19.3 per cent of the households having 5 members. Around 16 per cent of the households had 4 members. In the education category, majority of the respondents (42.7 per cent) studied up to secondary education followed by 21.3 per cent of the respondents being illiterate. On the other hand, 18.7 per cent of the respondents studied up to primary education.

Table 1: Socio-economic Characteristics

Socio-economic Characteristics	*Frequency (N = 150)*	*Percentage (N = 100)*
Gender		
Male	101	67.3
Female	49	32.7
Age		
Less than 25	4	2.7
26 to 30	31	20.7
31 to 35	29	19.3
36 to 40	30	20.0
41 to 45	28	18.7
Above 45	28	18.7

Socio-economic Characteristics	*Frequency (N = 150)*	*Percentage (N = 100)*
Family size		
2 members	5	3.3
3 members	9	6.0
4 members	24	16.0
5 members	29	19.3
6 members	34	22.7
7 members	23	15.3
8 members	17	11.3
9 members	6	4.0
10 members	3	2.0
Education		
Illiterate	32	21.3
Primary	28	18.7
Secondary	64	42.7
Higher secondary	19	12.7
Diploma	4	2.7
Degree and above	3	2.0

Source: Field Survey.

Table 2 shows the impact of lockdown on construction workers in Tirupattur district. As far as the number of days lost due to lockdown is concerned, 8.7 per cent of the respondents had managed their lost days during lockdown by doing alternative work whereas majority of the respondents (46.7 per cent) lost more than 70 days due to the pandemic lockdown causing severe financial crisis in the households of construction workers. Around 31.3 per cent and 11.3 per cent of the respondents lost 66 to 70 days and 61 to 65 days, respectively during the COVID lockdown. With regard to wage loss, majority of the respondents (91.3 per cent) have lost their wages because of COVID lockdown whereas only 8.7 per cent of the respondents went for alternative work. As far as the amount of wage lost is concerned, the majority of respondents (31.3 per cent) lost a wage of above Rs. 50,000 during the three months of lockdown followed by 29.3 per cent and 24.7 per cent of the respondents losing wages around Rs. 40,001 to 45,000 and Rs. 45,001 to 50,000, respectively. As far as the reason for wage loss is concerned, majority of the respondents (90 per cent) responded that COVID lockdown is the reason for wage loss while only 10 per cent of the respondents stated that COVID lockdown is not the reason. In the last six months, majority of the respondents (23.3 per cent) lost 2 days of work due to sickness followed by 22.7 per cent of the respondents losing 1 day, 19.3 per cent of respondents losing 3 days, and only 8 per cent of the respondents losing 5 days of work, respectively in the last six months due to sickness.

Table 2: Lockdown and its Impact on Construction Workers

Lockdown Impacts	*Frequency (N = 150)*	*Percentage (N = 100)*
No. of days lost due to lockdown		
Alternative work	13	8.7
Less than 60 days	3	2.0
61 to 65 days	17	11.3
66 to 70 days	47	31.3
Above 70 days	70	46.7
Wage lost		
Yes	137	91.3
No	13	8.7
Wage lost in rupees		
Alternative work	13	8.7
Less than 40,000	9	6.0
40,001 to 45,000	44	29.3
45,001 to 50,000	37	24.7
Above 50,000	47	31.3
COVID as the reason for wage loss		
Yes	135	90.0
No	15	10.0
No. of days lost due to sickness in last 6 months		
No loss	24	16.0
1 day	34	22.7
2 days	35	23.3
3 days	29	19.3
4 days	16	10.7
5 days	12	8.0

Source: Field Survey.

Table 3 shows the household monthly expenditure in different categories during post-COVID lockdown. It reveals that in food expenditure category majority of the households (50 per cent) spent Rs. 1,000 to 2,500 for food alone followed by 44 per cent of the households spending Rs. 2,501 to 5,000 and 4.7 per cent of the households spending Rs. 5,001 to 7,500 per month. For clothing expenditure, majority of the households (56.7 per cent) spent Rs. 201 to 400 per month followed by 26 per cent of the households spending less than Rs. 200 and only 14.7 per cent of the households spending Rs. 401 to 600. As far as housing expenditure is concerned, majority of the households (41.3 per cent) spent Rs. 201 to 400 per month towards housing followed by 36.7 per cent of the households spending less than Rs. 200 and 15.3 per cent of the households spending Rs. 401 to 600. Only 2 per cent of the households spent Rs. 801 to 1000 for housing expenditure.

Table 3: Household Monthly Expenditure

Expenditures	*Frequency (N = 150)*	*Percentage (N = 100)*
Food Expenditure		
Nil	1	0.7
Rs. 1000 to 2500	75	50.0
Rs. 2501 to 5000	66	44.0
Rs. 5001 to 7500	7	4.7
Rs. 7501 to 10000	1	0.7
Clothing Expenditure		
Less than Rs. 200	39	26.0
Rs. 201 to 400	85	56.7
Rs. 401 to 600	22	14.7
Rs. 601 to 800	4	2.7
Housing Expenditure		
Less than Rs. 200	55	36.7
Rs. 201 to 400	62	41.3
Rs. 401 to 600	23	15.3
Rs. 601 to 800	7	4.7
Rs. 801 to 1000	3	2.0

Source: Field Survey.

The association between wage loss and socio-economic factors has been assessed using the Chi-square test in Table 4. The explanatory variables are household size, gender, age, education, housing status, COVID-19 pandemic, and number of days lost due to sickness of the construction workers. The outcome of association explores that each and all socio-economic variables are associated with wage loss. It can be noted that all the variables are statistically significant at 1 per cent level. Especially, COVID-19 pandemic is the main reason for construction workers' wage loss during the lockdown period from April to June 2020. A similar study by Celeste 2020 also found that the COVID-19 lockdown resulted in high rate of unemployment and wage loss for construction workers in India.

Table 4: Association between Wage Loss and Socio-economic Factors

Variables	*Chi-Square*	*df*	*P value*	*Sig*
Household size	62.52	8	.000	***
Gender	18.02	1	.000	***
Age	21.44	5	.001	***
Education	101.60	5	.000	***
Housing status	102.50	1	.000	***
COVID-19	96.00	1	.000	***
Sickness	17.92	5	.003	***

Source: Computed data.

Suggestions/Action Plan

Strict rules to be imposed on social distancing and wearing face masks. The government must immediately take stock of its existing health care infrastructure and see how long it can hold taking into account the current case, load, and its inevitable rise in the days ahead. The government should also implement a complete lockdown for a very short period of one to two weeks to undertake this survey. Oxygen supply to ICU beds need to be increased. To increase the pace of vaccination, significant increase in testing and training efforts should be made so that not many cases go undetected. Moreover, the government should appoint more medical officers, nurse staff, and health activists. As far as construction workers are concerned, the government should undertake more measures in terms of social welfare schemes like incentives, increasing their wage, medical benefits, insurance, and scholarship for their children. Majority of the construction workers live on their worksites therefore, it is suggested that construction workers welfare board and concerned state governments should take some steps for the welfare of them. In addition to this, researchers should be encouraged to conduct more studies on occupational health of construction workers to bring effective policy implications.

Conclusion

COVID-19 is a big disaster for mankind as many individuals lost their lives. The world is facing both economic and social problems, particularly the construction workers in the present study area, pushing towards debt crisis due to lockdown. In a country like India, the government should provide basic infrastructural facilities, develop more medical facilities, and provide appropriate compensation to the workers. This can, in turn, help to solve the problem of wage loss to the workers.

References

[1] T. Abraham (2020). 'COVID-19 Communication in India'. *Journal of communication in Healthcare*, 13(1), pp. 10–12.

[2] M. Bou Hatoum, A. Faisal, H. Nassereddine and H. Sarvari (2021). 'Analysis of COVID-19 Concerns Raised by the Construction Workforce and Development of Mitigation Practices'. *Frontiers in Built Environment*, 7, p. 66.

[3] A. Celeste (2020). 'The Lived Experiences of Construction Workers during Covid-19 Pandemic: In Suburban Case'. *South Asian Journal of Social Studies and Economics*, pp. 98–103.

[4] K.M. Fitzpatrick, C. Harris, and G. Drawve (2020). 'How Bad is It? Suicidality in the Middle of the COVID-19 Pandemic'. *Suicide and Life-Threatening Behavior*, 50(6), pp. 1241–1249.

[5] P. Gauttam, N. Patel, B. Singh, J. Kaur, V.K. Chattu, and M. Jakovljevic (2021). 'Public Health Policy of India and COVID-19: Diagnosis and Prognosis of the Combating Response'. *Sustainability*, 13(6), 3415.

[6] D.N. Gujarati, D.C. Porter and S. Gunasekar (2012). 'Basic econometrics'. Tata McGraw-Hill Education.

[7] B. Harris-White and A. Sinha (2007). 'Trade Liberalization and India's Informal Economy'. Oxford University Press.

[8] E. Hanna, B. Gough, and S. Markham (2020). 'Masculinities in the Construction Industry: A Double-edged Sword for Health and Well-being?' *Gender, Work, and Organisation*, 27(4), pp. 632–646.

[9] R.M. John (2008). 'Price Elasticity Estimates for Tobacco Products in India'. *Health policy and planning*, 23(3), pp. 200–209.

[10] K.P. Kannan and T.S. Paola (2007). 'Workers in the Informal Sector: Initiatives by India's National Commission for Enterprises in the Unorganised Sector (NCEUS)'. *International Lab. Rev.*, 146, 321.

[11] S. Majumder and D. Biswas (2021). 'COVID-19 Impacts Construction Industry: Now, Then, and Future'. In *COVID-19: Prediction, Decision-Making, and its Impacts*, Springer, Singapore, pp. 115–125.

[12] S. Selvaraju, M.S. Kumar, J.W.V. Thangaraj, T. Bhatnagar, V. Saravanakumar, C.P.G. Kumar, and Chennai COVID Sero-Surveillance Team (2021). 'Population-based serosurvey for severe acute respiratory syndrome coronavirus 2 transmission, Chennai, India'. *Emerging Infectious Diseases*, 27(2), 586.

[13] World Health Organization (2020). Coronavirus disease 2019 (COVID-19): Situation report, 73.

[14] https://tn.data.gov.in/

[15] https://msme.gov.in/national-commission-enterprises-un-organised-sectornceus/

CHAPTER 7

COVID-19 and Its Implications on Disaster Management – A Case Study of Tamil Nadu

K. NIRMALKUMAR[1] AND V. SIVASANKAR[2]

Abstract: *This paper examines the impacts of COVID-19 on Tamil Nadu's economy at macro perspective during the period of first lockdown from 31 March,2020 to 3 May,2020. The purpose of the lockdown was to prevent the spread of coronavirus. The state government of Tamil Nadu gradually relaxed the lockdown however, this relaxation was not applicable to containment zones. There are extensive studies exploring the effects of COVID-19 on the Indian economy. However, there are limited studies to explore the regional perspective. In this context, this study examines the COVID-19 on Tamil Nadu's economy. This study is based on secondary data and have been obtained from sources of Statistical Hand Books of Tamil Nadu, Tamil Nadu Economic Appraisal, and Centre for Monitoring Indian Economy. The period of the present study was from March 2020 to March 2021.*

Keywords: COVID-19, Lockdown, Income, Migrant Workers, Tamil Nadu

Introduction

In both the developed and developing countries, the COVID-19-induced lockdowns have caused interruptions in livelihoods of people. On March 23, 2020, India's Prime Minister declared a state of emergency. As a result, economic activities in the country were sacked affecting the livelihoods of the country's 1.3 billion people. The projections of Gross Domestic Product (GDP) for the first quarter (April-June 2020) were announced by the National Statistics Agency, indicating a negative economic growth of

[1] PhD Research Scholar, The Post-Graduate and Research Department of Economics, Muthurangam Government Arts College (Autonomous), Vellore. E-mail: nirmalkrishnan87@gmail.com

[2] Associate Professor, Department of Economics, School of Management, Pondicherry University, Pondicherry. E-mail: sivasankarjh@gmail.com

23 per cent. In addition, the construction industry experienced a 50 per cent decrease in growth, followed by the service sector (47 per cent), and the manufacturing sector (39 per cent). Agriculture and related industries, on the other hand, are growing at a rate of 3 per cent. Agriculture policy specialists provide a number of theories to explain the agricultural sector's resilience, including the pandemic's timing, early public policy responses, and the development of infrastructure for social transfers, among others (Mohan et al., 2020), (Jhajhria et al., 2020).

This paper is divided into five parts. The first part of the paper provides an insight on the economy of Tamil Nadu at contemporary periods. The second part of the paper deals with the level of COVID-19 cases in Tamil Nadu. The third part of the paper provides information about the economic implications of lockdown in Tamil Nadu. The fourth part of the paper deals with the state government's measures while the fifth part deals with the challenges on policy measures.

Current Status of Tamil Nadu's Economy

The state of Tamil Nadu has an area of 1,30,058 square kilometer and a total population of 7,21,47,030. The density of population of the state is 555 per square kilometer. The decennial growth of population from 2001 to 2011 is 15.61 per cent. The State Gross Domestic Product (SGDP) of Tamil Nadu is Rs. 15,07,91,798 crore in 2018-19 and among this the service sector provides the major contribution (52.23 per cent) followed by industry (32.98 per cent) and agriculture (12.78 per cent). In the disaggregated analysis, manufacturing sector has the key contribution (19.74 per cent) in SGDP (Tamil Nadu, 2019). Some of the major manufacturing industries are automobiles, electronics, engineering, garments, textiles, leather, pharmaceuticals, chemicals, paper industries, etc. The Annual Survey of Industries (2016-17) reported that the number of factories in Tamil Nadu is 37,220 and it provides employment to 24,08,282 people. The second major contribution towards the state GDP is by the real estate, ownership of dwelling and professional services (17.96 per cent), followed by trade, hotel, and restaurant (12.61 per cent), agriculture, forestry, and fishing (12.40 per cent), trade repair and service (11.16 per cent), and construction (11.14 per cent). However, the proportion of agriculture in SGDP has changed to 12.78 per cent and the workers engaged in agriculture in Tamil Nadu is around 42.1 per cent according to the 2011 Census (Census of India, 2011). Among the agricultural workers, 12.9 per cent are cultivators and 29.2 per cent are agricultural labourers. The household industrial workers are 4.2 per cent and other workers are around 53.7 per cent. Therefore, among the total workers, main workers are 85 per cent while the marginal workers are 15 per cent (The Hindu 2016).

With the governments declaring partial or total lockdowns, the global economy has come to a halt causing unparalleled social and economic suffering among the world's population. The public health crisis struck at a time when India's GDP was already dropping and unemployment was rising (Dev and Sengupta, 2020). The Periodic Labour Force Survey reveals that the unemployment rate in Tamil Nadu is higher than all India level. Rural unemployment in Tamil Nadu is around 6.4 per cent while the urban unemployment is 6.7 per cent, which is higher than rural unemployment. On the other hand, unemployment in rural India is 5.0 per cent while urban unemployment is 7.7 per cent. The unemployment rate among rural males in Tamil Nadu is 7.0 per cent while that of rural females is 5.5 per cent. On the other hand, the rural unemployment of males across India is 5.6 per cent while that of females is 3.5 per cent. The urban unemployment rate of males in Tamil Nadu is 6.0 per cent while India has 7.1 per cent. Similarly, the urban female unemployment rate in Tamil Nadu is 8.4 per cent while India has 9.9 per cent (PLFS, 2018).

Tamil Nadu is one of the states to reduce poverty sharply than the rest of the country. Poverty in Tamil Nadu is 11.3 per cent while across India it is 21.9 per cent in the year 2011-12, according to the Mixed Recall Period (Tamil Nadu, 2018). In the Human Development Index, Tamil Nadu is better than the rest of India in education and health status. Literacy rate in Tamil Nadu is 80.09 per cent and in this, male literacy is 86.77 per cent while female literacy is 73.44 per cent according to the 2011 Census (Census of India, 2011). Health indicators of Tamil Nadu is better than the rest of India. Birth rate in Tamil Nadu is 14.7 per thousand while in the rest of India has 20.0 per thousand.

The death rate in Tamil Nadu is 6.5 per thousand while in India it is 6.2 per thousand. The infant mortality rate in Tamil Nadu is 15 per thousand while in India it is 32 per thousand. The life expectancy at birth of Tamil Nadu was also better than that of all over India. In Tamil Nadu, the life expectancy at birth per person was 71.7 years where for males it was 69.9 years and for females it was 73.7 years. For India, the life expectancy per person was 69.0 years where for males it was 67.8 years and for females it was 70.4 years (Human Development, 2017). The number of primary health centers in rural areas was 1,806 while in the urban areas the number of primary health centers was 2,927 in 2017-18 (Directorate of Family Welfare in Tamil Nadu, 2020).

Total Number of COVID-19 Cases and Death Rate in Tamil Nadu

The first case of COVID-19 was registered in India on 30 January, 2020 while in Tamil Nadu the first case was registered on 7 March 2020. Tamil Nadu reported the second highest rate of positive cases, next to Maharashtra. Table 1 shows the number of positive COVID-19 cases in Tamil Nadu from April 2020 to March 2021 among males, females, and transgenders. The number of registered cases has increased over this period. It was 2,323 in April 2020 which increased to 8, 86,673 in March 2021. In the gender analysis, during the preliminary period, males had the highest proportion of positive cases which declined over this period. But on the other hand, the proportion of females was low in the initial stage which increased in the later period. In April 2020, 66.85 per cent of males were reported positive for COVID-19 while for females it was 33.15 per cent. However, in March 2021, the proportion of males was 60.38 per cent while that of females was 40.0 per cent.

Table 1: Positive COVID-19 Cases in Tamil Nadu

Month	*Male*		*Female*		*Transgender*	*Total*
	Numbers	*Percentage*	*Numbers*	*Percentage*	*Numbers*	
April/2020	1,553	66.85	770	33.15		2,323
May/2020	14,065	62.98	8,259	36.98	9	22,333
June/2020	55,502	61.55	34,644	38.42	21	90,167
July/2020	1,49,107	60.65	96,725	39.34	27	2,45,859
August/2020	2,58,370	60.36	1,69,642	39.63	29	4,28,041
September/2020	3,60,729	60.36	2,36,842	39.63	31	5,97,602
October/2020	4,37,290	60.36	2,87,200	39.64	32	7,24,522
November/2020	4,72,430	60.42	3,09,451	39.58	34	7,81,915
December/2020	4,94,355	60.43	3,23,625	39.56	34	8,18,014
January/2021	5,06,678	60.44	3,31,628	39.56	34	8,38,340
February/2021	5,14,514	60.42	3,36,993	39.57	35	8,51,542
March/2021	5,35,382	60.38	3,51,255	39.61	36	8,86,673

Source: Health and Family Welfare Department, Government of Tamil Nadu.

Table 2 shows the number of recovered and dead cases of COVID-19 from April 2020 to March 2021 in Tamil Nadu. In the initial stage, the number of discharged cases were low but still slightly higher than 50 per cent positive cases. In April 2020, there were 54.15 per cent discharge cases which improved to 96.77 per cent in March 2021. The death rate of positive cases indicates that the absolute number has increased over this period. The number of death cases were 27 in April 2020 which increased to 12,719 in March 2021.

Table 2: Number of Recovered and Dead COVID-19 Cases

Month	*Recovered/Discharged*			*Death*		
	Number	*Percentage*	*Growth Rate*	*Number*	*Percentage*	*Growth Rate*
April/2020	1,258	54.15		27	1.16	
May/2020	12,757	57.12	9.14	173	0.77	5.41
June/2020	50,074	55.53	2.93	1,201	1.33	5.94
July/2020	1,83,956	74.82	2.67	3,935	1.60	2.28
August/2020	3,86,141	90.21	1.1	7,322	1.71	0.86
September/2020	5,41,819	90.67	0.4	9,520	1.59	0.30
October/2020	6,91,236	95.41	0.28	11,122	1.54	0.17
November/2020	7,59,206	97.10	0.1	11,712	1.50	0.05
December/2020	7,97,391	97.48	0.05	12,122	1.48	0.04
January/2021	8,21,430	97.98	0.03	12,356	1.47	0.02
February/2021	8,35,024	98.06	0.02	12,496	1.47	0.01
March/2021	8,58,075	96.77	0.03	12,719	1.43	0.02

Source: Health and Family Welfare Department, Government of Tamil Nadu.

Testing is an important mechanism to reduce the spread of diseases. The number of COVID-19 testing centers in Tamil Nadu is 237 which include 67 government centers and 170 private centers (Health and Family Welfare, 2020). The state of Tamil Nadu has the highest number of testing centers and the highest number of tests were conducted here compared to any other state in India. Table 3 shows the number of samples tested and the number of positive cases. The number of samples tested has increased and as result the number of positive cases has Census of India 2011) also increased. In March 2020, the number of COVID-19 tests conducted were 2,354 while the number of registered positive cases was 124. The state government instigated to speed up the testing centers and samples. It was 1, 95,95,368 tests in March 2021 the number of positive cases was 8,86,673.

Table 3: Samples Tested and Number of Positive Samples in Tamil Nadu

Month	*Number of Sample Tested*	*Number of Sample Positive*
March 2020	2,354	124
April 2020	1,19,748	2,323
May 2020	4,91,962	22,333
June 2020	11,70,683	90,167
July 2020	26,58,138	2,45,859
August 2020	48,13,147	4,28,041
September 2020	73,54,050	5,97,602
October 2020	99,56,210	7,24,522
November 2020	1,20,60,001	7,81,915
December 2020	1,41,91,494	8,18,014
January 2021	1,60,19,962	8,38,340
February 2021	1,74,79,572	8,51,542
March 2021	1,95,95,368	8,86,673

Source: Health and Family Welfare Department, Government of Tamil Nadu

Lockdown and Its Implications on Tamil Nadu's Economy

The Government of India had announced its first lockdown on 25 March 2020 which was followed by three more lockdowns proclaimed by the union government. The first phase of lockdown was from 25 March 2020 to 14 April 2020, second phase from 15 April 2020 to 3 May 2020, third phase from 4 May 2020 to 17 May 2020 and the fourth phase from 18 May 2020 to 31 May 2020. These different phases of lockdown completely shut down all economic activities and it severely hit the economic growth. The lockdowns also created severe economic troubles to all sections of people. The union government of India and different state governments announced several packages to revive the economic growth of India. This unintended lockdown created panic among migrant workers in India. Urban migrant workers are unskilled workers and they usually worked in casual or contractual types of work in manufacturing units, construction sites, hotels, and restaurants. This lockdown led to stoppage in all factories and construction activities and it created rapid unemployment in India. While the epidemic has impacted livelihoods throughout India's socioeconomic strata, those in the unorganized sector, which accounts for 86 per cent of the workforce, have been hit the hardest as they struggle to satisfy basic needs while dealing with the risk of infection (ILO, 2020).

According to Centre for Monitoring Indian Economy (CMIE), the unemployment rate of Tamil Nadu in March 2020 was 8.8 per cent and it abruptly increased to 23.5 per cent in April 2020, 21.7 per cent in May 2020, slightly declined to 33.2 per cent in May 2020, 12.2 per cent in June 2020, 6.8 per cent in July 2020, 2.6 per cent in August 2020, and 3.0 per cent in March 2021. During the lockdown period, the level of unemployment rate in Tamil Nadu was higher than that of all over India, as shown in Table 4. However, the rate of unemployment gradually reduced after the relaxation of lockdowns. During the lockdown period, Tamil Nadu had higher unemployment rate than that of all over India. In April 2020, all India unemployment rate was 23.5 per cent while in Tamil Nadu it was 49.8 per cent. Similarly, in May 2020 and June 2020 there was a higher level of unemployment as compared to all over India (CMIE, 2020).

Table 4: Unemployment Rate in Tamil Nadu and India

Month/Year	*Tamil Nadu (%)*	*All India (%)*
March 2020	6.4	8.8
April 2020	49.8	23.5
May 2020	33.2	21.7
June 2020	12.2	10.2
July 2020	6.8	7.4
August 2020	2.6	8.3
September 2020	5.0	6.7
October 2020	2.2	7.0
November 2020	1.1	6.5
December 2020	0.5	9.1
January 2021	4.0	6.5
February 2021	4.8	6.9
March 2021	3.0	6.5

Source: Centre for Monitoring Indian Economy

The lockdowns have directly affected three major sectors in Tamil Nadu which includes Micro, Small, and Medium Enterprises (MSMEs), construction sector, and restaurant and hotel industry. The number of registered micro, small, and medium enterprises in Tamil Nadu are 12.89 lakh and the share of Tamil Nadu at the national level is 15.07 per cent. The number of registered entrepreneurs is around 20.13 lakh. The micro, small, and medium enterprises provide employment to around 128.91 lakh people and the total investment in 2019 was Rs. 2,23,783.75 crore. The major micro, small, and medium enterprises are textile, electronic products, engineering products, auto ancillaries, leather products, chemicals, plastic, garments, and jewellery. In the special distribution of micro, small, and medium enterprises, majority are located in the northern and western parts of Tamil Nadu. The northern industrial cluster consists of Chennai, Kancheepuram, Thiruvallur, and Vellore districts. This north and western industrial cluster accounts for 71 per cent of micro, small, and medium enterprises. The northern parts alone account for 33.7 per cent of micro, small, and medium enterprises while Chennai and Kancheepuram alone account for 17.5 per cent and 7.45 per cent, respectively (Tamil Nadu, 2019).

The widespread of COVID-19 has wreaked havoc on all sectors including micro, small, and medium businesses. The untested lockdowns suffocated the micro, small, and medium enterprises' economic activities, causing unfavorable shock such as lack of acquiring raw materials, decreased production, delivery of finished products, and a lack of workers to work in the manufacturing process. The effects are numerous including job loss, reduced revenue production, decreased sales, and a fall in working-class income (Hariharan et al., 2021). The government has primarily implemented emergency stimulus and preventive measures to protect micro, small, and medium enterprises including funding to address cash flow issues, job preservation through various schemes, and business processes as well as measures to widen trade opportunities by establishing their capacities (Chauhan, 2020; WTO, 2020).

In addition to this Special Economic Zones (SEZs), all major software companies, automobile industries like Hyundai, Ford, Nissan, Enfield, etc., located in Chennai and Kancheepuram. Thiruvallur accounts for 5.93 per cent of micro, small, and medium enterprises which consists of engineering and textile industries. Vellore accounts for 2.4 per cent of micro, small, and medium enterprises which is well-known for its leather industrial cluster. The western part accounts for 37.6 per cent of micro, small, and medium enterprises. The western industrial cluster consists of Coimbatore, Tiruppur, Erode, Salem, Karur, and Krishnagiri. Coimbatore district accounts for 11.5 per cent and Tiruppur accounts for 10.5 per cent of micro, small, and medium enterprises in Tamil Nadu. These western belts of micro, small, and medium enterprises include knit wear, cotton, and handloom industries. These manufacturing sectors observe all varieties of labour like skilled, semi-skilled, and unskilled labour (Industries Department, 2020).

The majority of labourers are contractual and casual labour. This labour is migrant in nature, both within the state of Tamil and other states. The other states to which these labourers may migrate include Andhra Pradesh, Odisha, Uttar Pradesh, Jharkhand, Chhattisgarh, Bihar, West-Bengal, and Assam. Moreover, the micro, small, and medium enterprises sector was already damaged due to demonetisation and Goods and Service Tax. This lockdown further escalated to damage micro, small, and medium enterprises. Many workers lost their employment and wages and as a result their income as well. Consequently, they were pushed to hunger. During lockdown, the Tamil Nadu government announced free distribution of rice and grocery items to ration card holders but this failed as majority of migrant workers did not have ration cards (Wire, 2020a).

The second major employment providing sector in Tamil Nadu is construction sector and the share of construction to the state's gross domestic product is 11 per cent. This sector observes unskilled labour. Construction activities in Chennai fully depend on migrant labour. Generally, non-Tamil migrant construction workers are used public road construction activities including construction of bridges, business, and commercial complex establishments. Tamil migrant workers are used in individual houses and small business establishments. Major causes for exhausting north Indian labour in the construction activities are low wages and long working hours.

According to the domestic workers' survey, labourers are in a poor position, with no assurance of income during the lockdown and an absence of an united front to demand government social security and other benefits. Only a small percentage of them undertake odd casual labour, leaving the others to fend for themselves (Godsen and Nirmalkumar, 2021). Migrant workers are paid Rs. 400 to Rs. 600 while Tamil workers are paid Rs. 700 to Rs. 900. In the working hours, Tamil workers only worked for 8 hours while north Indian workers did for 15 hours. The migrant labourers were forced to return to their villages without income. Construction workers also returned to their villages to engage in agricultural work. This process increased the underemployment and unemployment in rural areas of Tamil Nadu (Wire, 2020).

The northern and western parts of micro, small, and medium enterprises abundantly depend upon migrant workers. The number of non-Tamil Migrant in Tamil Nadu is 10,76,506 and according to the district wise distribution of migrant labour, Kancheepuram district has 2.23 lakh (20.9 per cent), Chennai accounts for 1.94 lakh (18.2 per cent), Thiruvallur accounts for 1.3 lakh (12.2 per cent), Coimbatore accounts for 1.29 lakh (12.1 per cent), Tiruppur accounts for 96.248 thousand (9 per cent), and Krishnagiri accounts for 84.987 (7.9 per cent). In the sectoral distribution of migrant labour in Tamil Nadu, the manufacturing sectors account for 2.88 lakh labourers followed by textile with 1.5 lakh labourers, constructions account for 1.21 lakh, hotel and restaurants account for 98.03 thousand, small business establishment account for 94.235 thousand, service activities account for 83.280 thousand, security accounts for 43.294 thousand, transport accounts for 39.328 thousand and bricks industry and hawkers account for 21.208 thousand. During the lockdown, all migrant workers lost their employment and many migrant workers reported that they were not paid their wages for March and April 2020. Moreover, migrant workers in the special economic zones worked without wage for 40 days during the 5 lockdown. Some industries forced their workers to live in temporary huts without basic amenities. Migrant workers were forced to return to their native villages or residence and as a result labour scarcity arose in manufacturing units (Wire, 2020a).

The third largest share of Tamil Nadu's gross domestic product and employment is provided by the hotels and restaurants industry. This lockdown led to shutting down of hotels and restaurants. Due to absence of transportation, the entire supply chain in agriculture has collapsed. On one side, the farmers were not able to continue farming activities due to non-availability of inputs. On the other hand, harvested agricultural commodities were not being sold due to the absence of transportation. Finally, the lockdown severely affected production in agriculture, manufacturing, and service sectors in Tamil Nadu's economy. Tamil Nadu also has the second largest costal line next to Gujarat and it shares 13 districts. The share of marine fish in Tamil Nadu is 10 to 12 per cent of the national fish production. More than 2 million people are engaged in fishing activity who suffered during the lockdown due to fish processing industry being closed. Consequently, the fishing communities were also affected (Wire, 2020b).

Government Measures

This section deals on different relief measures made by Tamil Nadu Government during the lockdown period has follows:

Relief Package to All Ration Card Holders and Differently Abled People

The Tamil Nadu government announced a Rs. 3,280 crore relief package providing financial assistance of Rs. 1,000 to all ration card holders. It included free of 20 kilogram of rice, 1 kilogram of sugar, 1 kilogram of dhal and cocking oil for April, May and June 2020. The number of ration card holders in Tamil Nadu is around 2 crore and almost all ration card holders availed this benefit. A cash assistance of Rs. 1,500 was provided to differently abled people. The government of India COVID-19 also provided cash assistance under the social assistant package which has greatly supported families, especially small and marginal farmers who are vulnerable (Varshney et al., 2021). However, the question is whether the cash benefits provided by the Tamil Nadu government was adequate for all families (Sivasankar, 2021).

Relief Package for Unorganised Workers

Another major important financial package provided by the Tamil Nadu state government was financial assistance of Rs. 1,000 to the unorganised workers. At present, 17 different types of unorganised welfare boards exist in Tamil Nadu. The number of unorganised workers in Tamil Nadu is 14.07 lakh and among these construction workers are around 2 lakhs. (Sivasankar, 2021) Domestic violence at households, increasing job load at households, health care access concerns and other issues have also increased among informal domestic women workers during the COVID-19 period (Sumalatha et al., 2021). Unfortunately, in this case, social security law is ineffective for informal sector employees which includes laws like the Employees State Insurance Act 1948, Workman's Compensation Act 1923, Building and Construction Workers Act 1996, Industrial Disputes Act 1947, and others focusing solely on various types of social security and welfare aid for organised sector workers. Although some have argued that these requirements apply to the informal sector as well, the fact remains that the current law applies only to 8 per cent of India's 459 million workforce (Srivastava, 2020). In this situation, only the workers who are member of the Tamil Nadu informal workers welfare board have available for this benefit. Moreover, in the absence of social security for informal workers, it seems that their economy and health have been severely affected during the COVID-19 period (ILO, 2020).

Relief Package for Micro, Small, and Medium Enterprises

The Tamil Nadu government announced a new scheme called the COVID-19 relief and development scheme. This scheme facilitates to around 2,000 micro, small, and medium enterprises who have availed loans from the Tamil Nadu Industrial Investment Corporation (TIIC). The scheme will be executed with a fund of Rs. 200 crore (Sivasankar, 2021). During COVID-19, most of the micro, small, and medium enterprises were having difficulty in acquiring financing and promoting their products (Behera et al., 2021). Production, employment and income of small and medium enterprise have been severely affected during the COVID-19 period so it is necessary for the government to formulate policies for the recovery of the micro, small, and medium enterprises sector.

Relief Package to Agricultural Communities

Tamil Nadu has also announced a three-month moratorium (till June 30 2020) for the repayment of installments on crop loans, house loans, etc., and payment of certain charges for the following categories: payment of wealth tax and water tax to local bodies. The COVID-19 relief findings imply that the fungibility of money obtained through government transfer packages were important in reducing credit limitations and enhancing agricultural input spending. Farmers that have benefited from the Pradhan Mantri Garib Kalyan Yojana plan spent significantly more on the procurement of seeds, pesticides, and fertilisers. The release of cash transfers demonstrated that emergency assistance packages have reached India's most vulnerable people in the society (Varshney et al., 2021).

Constitute High Level Committee

The Tamil Nadu Government has formed a high-level committee with 24 coordinator members led by former Reserve Bank of India (RBI) Governor C. Rengarajan to assess the immediate impact of the COVID-19 pandemic on the state's economy. The committee is mandated with devising strategies to re-energise the state's fiscal position.

Challenges Faced by Tamil Nadu's Economy

Tamil Nadu has gone under heavy financial crises. Therefore, to generate additional income it relies on two sources: first one is to open liquor shops and the second one is to hike petrol prices. The average per day sale of liquor is around 90 crore. In 2018-19, liquor generated a revenue of Rs. 31,157.83 crore. After lockdown, the first day sale was around Rs. 170 crore. This year 2021 government of Tamil Nadu has targeted a sale of Rs. 33,000 core and almost achieved it in May. The second source of income was to increase petrol and diesel prices. By midnight of 3 May 2020, the Value Added Tax (VAT) on petrol and diesel was increased as Rs. 3.25 and Rs. 2.50, respectively. This generated additional income of 250 crore per month. This value added tax does not come under GST ambit and this lead to inflation of food prices, particularly vegetables The Tamil Nadu government wanted to reduce the fiscal stress and save 750 crore. This was achieved through ban on new posts which led to an increase in educated unemployment. In addition to this, a ban on dearness allowance and earning leave benefits for all government employees and pensioners was also implemented. It reduced the purchasing power of the working classes. The retirement age of government employees was also increased from 58 years to 59 years. The reason for the increasing age limit was that the state government was unable to settled pension benefits (Sivasankar, 2021).

Suggestions

- Since many states still have wage and income inequalities, the government should guarantee that a minimum wage legislation is enacted at the state level. The present economic plan must be fulfilled by the actual world situation. The lower middle and lower class households must be encouraged to maximise their consumption through effective revenue earning.
- Government policy decisions must be made to increase their savings for migrant workers and unskilled workers to improve their social security and livelihoods.
- Income, employment, investment, and production in Tamil Nadu have declined sharply during the period of international expansion and it is necessary to increase savings to recover from these. The Government of Tamil Nadu is required to spend only on essential departments.
- Tamil Nadu informal workers union can play an active role, with the support of the civil society, to mobilise and organise domestic workers to claim their rightful entitlements from the government has announced assistance to the workers through the Tamil Nadu informal workers union which has not been received by many workers till now.

Conclusion

To combat COVID-19, increased testing capabilities, guidance for universal mask usage, and social distancing should all work together. Above all, India should be adequately prepared to deal with any epidemic that may occur in the future (Arun and Premkumar, 2021). From April 2020 to March 2021, 8,86,673 people were infected with COVID-19 in Tamil Nadu. Out of these, 12,619 died. The financial condition of Tamil Nadu has gradually deteriorated during the COVID-19 period. The industrial sector in Tamil Nadu has been badly affected while the rest of the agricultural and services sectors have been moderately affected. Fixing these can be challenging. During the lockdown period, Tamil Nadu had higher unemployment rate than all over India. In April, all India unemployment rate was 23.5 per cent while in Tamil Nadu it was 49.8 per cent.

References

[1] J.V. Arun, and A. Premkumar (2021). 'Estimating the Role of Climatologic Factors during COVID-19 Outbreak in Chennai', In V. Sivasankar and J. V. Arun, *COVID-19 in Tamil Nadu Repercussions and the Avenues Ahead*. Michigan, USA: MANAK Publication, pp. 151–63.

[2] M. Behera, S. Mishra, N. Mohapatra, and A. R. Behera, (2021). 'COVID-19 Pandemic and Micro, Small, and Medium Enterprises (MSMEs): Policy Response for Revival', *Small Enterprises Development, Management & Extension Journal*, pp. 213–28.

[3] J.P. Chauhan, (2020). 'An Impact of COVID-19 on Indian Economy: A Brief View of Selected Sectors', *EPRA International Journal of Multidisciplinary Research (IJMR)*, pp. 9–12.

[4] CMIE, Center for Monitering Indian Economy (2020), 'Unemployment Report, Mumbai: Center for Monitoring Indian Economy'. Retrieved from https://www.cmie.com/ accessed on 3 March 2021.

[5] M.S. Dev and R. Sengupta (2020). *COVID-19: Impact on the Indian Economy* (*Working Paper*). India: Indira Gandhi Institute of Development Research, Mumbai, India. Retrieved from https://ideas.repec.org/p/ind/igiwpp/2020-013 html, accessed on 6 March 2021.

[6] M. Godsen and K. Nirmalkumar (2021). 'COVID-19 and Domestic Workers in Vellore Town', in V. Sivasankar, and J. Arun, *COVID-19 in Tamil Nadu Repercussions and the Avenues Ahead*, Michigan, USA: Manak Publication, pp. 173–82.

[7] A. Hariharan, S.Thomas, and P.Viswanathan, (2021). 'Impact of COVID-19 on the Performance of Imco, Small and Medium Enterprises (MSMEs) in India: A Case Study in Kerala', *Annals of RSCB*, pp. 14797–816.

[8] Health and Family Welfare, D. (2020). *COVID-19 Daily Bulletin.* Chennai: Government of Tamil Nadu.

[9] Human Development, I. (2017). *Tamil Nadu Human Development Report.* Chennai, Tamil Nadu: State Planning Commission.

[10] Jhajhria, A. Kandpal, S.J. Balaji., J. Jumrani, I.T. Kingsly, K. Kumar, N.P. Singh, P.S. Birthal, P. Sharma, R. Saxena, S. Srivastava, S.P. Subash, S. Pal, and V. Nikam (2020). *COVID-19 Lockdown and India Agriculture: Options to Reduce the Impact.* India: National Institute of Agricultural Economics and Policy Research, Indian Council of Agricultural Research Working Paper.

[11] V. Mohan, D.K. Desh, R. Mahesh, and I. Aujila (2020). 'How Agriculture Sayed Resilient Despite COVID Shock', India: *Times of India.* Retrieved from https://timesofindia.indiatimes.com/india/how-agriculture-stayed-resilient-despite-covid-shock/articleshow/76083960.cms, accessed on 30 May 2020.

[12] PLFS (2018). *Periodic Labour Force Surveys,* New Delhi, India: Government of India, Ministry of Statistics and Programme Implementation. Retrieved from https://pib.gov.in/PressReleaseIframePage.aspx?PRID=162936, accessed on 05 September 2020.

[13] V. Sivasankar (2021). 'COVID-19 Lockdown and its Economics Implication in Tamil Nadu: A Macro View', in V. Sivasankar and J. Arun, *COVID-19 in Tamil Nadu Repercussions and the Avenues Ahead.* Michigan, USA: Manak Publication Pvt. Ltd, pp. 1-14.

[14] S.C. Srivastava (2020). 'Impact of COVID-19 on Labourers of Unorganised Sector', *Indian Journal of Society and Politics*, pp. 69-72.

[15] B.S. Sumalatha, D, L. Bhat, and K.P. Chitra (2021). 'Impact of COVID-19 on Informal Sector: A Study of Women Domestic Workers in India', *The Indian Economic Journal*, pp. 441-61.

[16] Tamil Nadu, Economic Appraisal (2018). *Tamil Nadu Economic Appraisals.* Chennai: Department of Evaluation and Applied Research. Retrieved from https://www.direar.tn.gov.in/, accessed on 10 November 2020.

[17] Tamil Nadu Government (2019). *Statistical Hand Book, Department of Economics and Statistics (For Various Other Years).* Tamil Nadu: Department of Economics and Statistics Government of Tamil Nadu. Retrieved from https://tn.data.gov.in/catalog/statistical-hand-book-2019-area-and-population#web_catalog_tabs_block_10, accessed on 19 October 2020D.

[18] Varshney, A. Kumar, A.K. Mishra, S. Rashid, and P.K. Joshi (2021). 'India's COVID-19 Social Assistance Package and its Impact on the Agriculture Sector', *Agricultural System*, pp. 1–11.

[19] WTO (2020). 'Helping MSMEs Navigate the COVID-19 Crisis', *WTO (Hq): Helping MSMEs Navigate the COVID-19 Crisis*. World Trade

Organisation. Retrieved from https://www.wto.org/english/tratop_e/covid19_e/msmes_report_e.pdf, accessed on 24 September 2020.

[20] Government of Tamil Nadu (2013-14), *Tamil Nadu – An Economic Appraisal*, Department of Evaluation and Applied Research. Retrieved from http://www.tn.gov.in/dear/index.htm, accessed on 28 November 2020.

[21] International Labour Organisation (ILO) (2020a). *Domestic Workers and the COVID-19 Pandemic Understanding Challenges Ahead and Evolving Collective Strategies*, Retrieved from https://www.ilo.org/wcmsp5/groups/public/—asia/—robangkok/—sro new_delhi/documents/meetingdocument/wcms_748030.pdf , accessed on 26 December 2020.

[22] International Labour Organisation (ILO) (2020b). *ILO Monitor: COVID-19 and the World of Work.* 2nd edition updated estimates and analysis. Retrieved from https://www.ilo.org/wcmsp5/groups/public/@dgreports/@dcomm/documents/briefingnote/wcms_740877.pdf, accessed on 07 April 2020.

[23] Industries Department (2020). Major Industries, Policy Note, Minister for Industries, Government of Tamil Nadu 2020. Retrieved from https://www.tn.gov.in/documents/category/2/2020-2021, accessed on 8 March 2021.

[24] Ministry of Health and Family Welfare, Government of India (2020). 'COVID-19 Bulletin, Government of India'. Retrieved from https://www.mohfw.gov.in/, accessed on 14 March 2021.

[25] *The Hindu* (2016), 'Fewer Cultivators, form Labourers in TN', Retrieved from https://www.thehindu.com/news/national/tamil-nadu/fewer-cultivators-farm-labourers-in-tn/article4769431.ece, accessed on 5 January 2021.

[26] Wire (2020), 'You Can't go Back: Migrant Workers Told in Tamil Nadu', *The Wire*, Retrieved from https://thewire.in/labour/you-cant-go-back-migrant-workers-in-tamil-nadu, accessed on 09 May 2020.

[27] Wire (2020a), 'Perception, Legality and Politics of the Migrant Worker Crisis in Lockdown', *The Wire*, Retrieved from https://thewire.in/labour/migrant-worker-crisis-lockdown, accessed on 15 May 2020.

[28] Wire (2020b), 'Afraid and Confused, Tamil Nadu's Fisherman Suffer as Lockdown Ravages Their Livelihoods', *The Wire*, Retrieved from https://thewire.in/rights/tamil-nadu-fishermen-lockdown, accessed on 18 April 2020.

CHAPTER 8

COVID-19 Pandemic Outbreak and Food Service Industry: A Case Study of Coimbatore Restaurants

P. Raja[1], Ankathi Raghu[2] and Sivakami V.[3]

Abstract: *Food service industry (FSI) was one of the hardest hit during the outbreak of Corona Virus Disease 2019 (COVID-19) as they were shut down to control the spread of virus across the society. The FSI is a labour- intensive industry, as it requires huge manpower at every stage, from preparation to the delivery of services. The COVID-19 pandemic almost nullified the organised and unorganised restaurant business across the country. Dining out being one of the most popular social activity in a metropolitan city like Coimbatore (popularly known as Manchester of South India), the city has branches of popular restaurant chains, from across the globe. Also being the gateway to western ghats, the city attracts tourists all over the year and generates more revenue to the FSI industry. Measures such as lockdown, social distancing, and dine-in restrictions adopted by the government to slow down the spread of virus, has imparted huge loss to the FSI that has in turn severely affected the livelihood of millions of restaurant workers in the country with Coimbatore being no exception. In this background, the authors have studied the case of impact of COVID-19 on restaurants with special reference to Coimbatore. Primary data from restaurants were used for this study. The findings based on the data provide a significant contribution to the FSI and identify the factors that need to be tapped to frame a strategy to increase the sales volume in upcoming pandemic alike situations. Also, the authors have suggested to follow Standard Operating procedure (SOP) instructed by the government even after the pandemic, which may improve the good will of the organisation.*

[1] Assistant Professor, The Department of Tourism and Hospitality Management, Central University of Tamil Nadu, Thiruvarur.

[2] Associate Professor, The Department of Tourism and Hospitality Management, Central University of Tamil Nadu, Thiruvarur.

[3] Guest Faculty, The Department of Tourism and Hospitality Management, Central University of Tamil Nadu, Thiruvarur.

Keywords: Food Service Industry, COVID-19, Global Economy, Risk Factors, Hospitality Business

Introduction

Food Service Industry is diverse encompassing fast food outlets, self-service cafeterias, motorway service stations, restaurants, bistros, cafés, ethnic restaurants of all styles, hotels of all classes, and motels. Players in the business describe FSI as being in the midst of a perfect storm because of its tremendous growth in the worldwide market. The restaurant and food industry is part of the hotel industry and plays an important role in the tourism industry. FSI is a part of the lodging and tourist industry, although it has its own distinct qualities. Restaurants, takeaways, and even contract catering are more dynamic, changing, and fashion-prone than hotels or tourist destinations. The FSI's principal objective is to regulate the sale of food and beverages provided in paper, plastic, or other disposable containers for immediate consumption inside, outside, or away from a structure, as well as enterprises that provide food delivery for quick consumption. The term 'restaurant' refers to a wide range of establishments and culinary techniques. Apart from the basic function of the human condition, which is—to eat, visiting a restaurant is, and always has been, much more than fulfilling (Almeida et al., 2015; Santich, 2005). Dining at a restaurant has always been a social experience and an occasion to meet old friends, with food presented on the table, and to even be entertained by a small musical ensemble. However, FSI is vulnerable and delicate to natural hazards such as the COVID-19 pandemic and any resultant economic shock (Kalaivani and Girija, 2018).

India is known for its diverse cuisines, which play an important role in the social structure, way of life, and culture. Dining with family, relatives, and friends is an excellent method to become more acquainted with one's culture. Ever since urbanisation, FSI has identified its place in metropolitan cities (Vig and Agarwal, 2021). India is the second-most populous country in the world. Career-driven individuals of the country with global exposure, more disposable income, and diverse eating habits prefer dining out to have exceptional experiences when compared to the previous generation. Gastronomic lovers are now willing to afford convenience, experience, and ambiance. Recent research studies have also shown that there has been an increasing trend among the Indians to taste various dishes pertaining to a different region. This has also led to an increase in regional and international delicacies in FSI.

The COVID-19 pandemic has affected the global economy severely. According to MacDonald et al., 2020, domestic consumption of food services at restaurants make up, on average, almost 4 per cent of GDP in G20 economies, with a minimum of about 2 per cent in Mexico. This explains a strident decline in the activity in FSI and its significant negative effects on all countries, as shown in (Graph 1). FSI contributes to the employment sector significantly. Accommodation and FSI jointly contribute about 5 per cent of workers, on an average, among G20 countries. An intense decline in visits to restaurants has been marked between March and May 2020. Table reservation in FSI has almost nullified (99 per cent) worldwide during the peak lockdowns and had only recovered, on an average, to about 60 per cent of their 2019 bookings by the end of June, as lockdowns eased. However, with a partially compensating effect, FSI was never completely closed. Despite strict social distancing policies being in place, restaurants were permitted to operate takeaways and own delivery services.

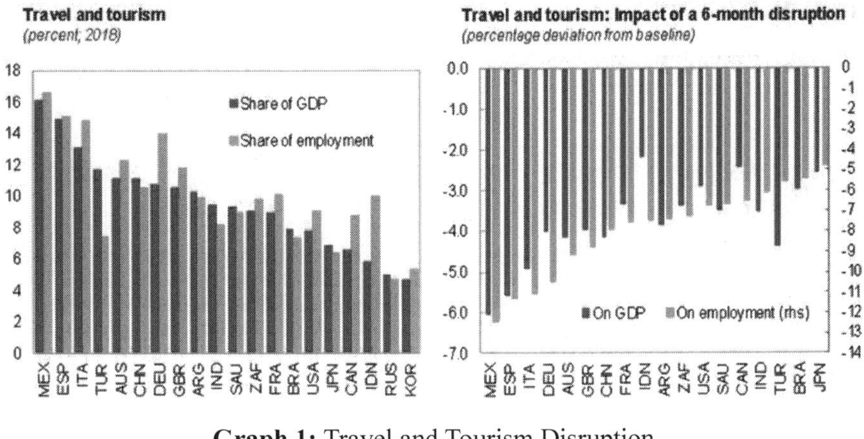

Graph 1: Travel and Tourism Disruption

Source: MacDonald et al. (2020), 'A Simple Guide to Estimating the Impact of COVID-19 on Travel and Hospitality Activity', *IMF – Special Series on COVID-19.*

A nationwide lockdown due to COVID-19 has impacted India's food service industry negatively. The Federation of Hotel and Restaurant Association of India (FHRAI), estimated that 70 per cent of the overall hospitality establishments in the country have shut down in the absence of support from the government which led to a significant crisis in India. During the curfew, only essential services were allowed to operate. Restaurants closed their operations completely during the first phase of lockdown, to curb the virus' spread in the country. But once the curfew was lifted, FSI could not commence the dine-in services right away, and only takeaway orders were allowed from the premises. Government officers relaxed the limitations after 6 months, by permitting a dine-in facility at premises with reduced capacities and maintaining social distancing norms. After the reopening, the recovery has been very gradual.

Background and Objectives

Coimbatore is a city with a pleasing climate and industries like textiles, electric motors, pumps, automobile spares, iron steel, and aluminum costing from the major exports that attract all kinds of tourists towards the destination. The city is also known for its educational institutions with a great reputation. With a high per-capita income of consumers, high standard of living, and changes in the lifestyle of people, more and more consumers flock to various restaurants to achieve social gatherings. The high expenditure level of the locals enables them to have an active food culture (weekend dining, get together, etc.) has ultimately led to the growth of restaurants that serve regional and international delicacies with numerous cuisine options for dining. Coimbatore district being the second hardest pandemic hit by the pandemic in Tamil Nadu, after Chennai, faced an economic crisis that caused financial imbalances and risks especially over the business of FSI. The key issue considered for the present study is the change of consumption pattern with business restrictions like weekend lockdown, time restrictions during weekdays, restricted dine-in facility, and social distancing norms posed by the government. Thus, the current study was undertaken with an objective to explore the behavioral and consumption pattern, sales pattern, and volume of famous organised chain restaurants from the city during pandemic and post-pandemic situation.

Methodology of the Study

Secondary data from April 2020 to October 2021 was collected from the branch of an organised restaurant chain in Coimbatore city with an undertaking of not disclosing the name of the restaurant. Secondary data collected from this restaurant includes methods of selling, type of orders, average bill values, and cost incurred by the restaurant in the city during the study period. The findings of the study are based on a branch of restaurant that is recognised as an organised business sector and is located in heart of the city, Findings may differ within an unorganised restaurant chain outlet and location of the restaurant. Also, the study has not disclosed the name of the restaurant, since it will be an advantage for a competitor to understand the sales strategy of the restaurant.

Review of Literature

This section highlights the scenario of restaurant business, behavioural changes of customers during and post COVID-19 by various authors and organisations related to hospitality industry.

Restaurant Business during COVID-19

The World Health Organisation (WHO) declared COVID-19 as pandemic on 11 March, 2020. Severson and Bellany (2020), stated that a major crisis has struck the hospitality business, including accommodation sector, food service, and bars. It is believed that half of the restaurants will not survive therefore, making a strategy to maintain consumer demand is critical (Sigala, 2020). Statistica (2020) predicted that COVID-19 caused 100.08 million employment loss in travel and tourism industry worldwide. The recent novel corona virus generated a global anxiety in the first half of January 2020 and by the end of December 2020 the virus had infected millions of people globally. The restaurant industry appears particularly vulnerable to a long crisis. Bartik et al., (2020) identified that FSI seems specifically vulnerable to a long crisis. According to their study restaurateurs believed that they had a 72 per cent chance of survival if the crisis lasts for a month, 30 per cent if it lasts for four months, and only 15 per cent if the crisis lasts for six months. This indicated that unorganised sectors can easily fall down due to significant crises, such as the COVID-19 pandemic. Internal (poor management, poor service, and low-quality products) or external (economic, political, and health issues) crises in FSI can be solved with corrective measures but the industry does not have control over the business environment and must rely on government support and measures to overcome the crisis (Parsa et al., 2011; Jung S and Jang S, 2019). According to the studies of Jung S and Jang S (2019) and Wang Y (2009), at times of crisis or post-crisis, competitiveness among market players increases as demand decreases.

Behavioural Changes Due to the New Normal and Government Measures

The food service industry is exposed to health crises such as pandemics as there are immense interaction and gatherings among family, friends and relatives (Yang et al., 2020). This vulnerability of FSI is likely to result from behavioral changes in response to the crises. COVID-19 pandemic has significantly altered the day-to-day life activities and introduced a 'new normal' that forced socio-economic and behavioural changes in the absence of medical facility, treatment, and vaccinations (Baum and Hai, 2020). While practising the 'new normal', people had an increasing tendency towards avoiding the dine-in services, thereby avoiding physical contact with people as the walk-in customers are worried and concerned with safety issues throughout the food consumption process (Pressman et al., 2020). The food service industry called for touch less service, which is believed to refrain spread of infections significantly. One of the distinctive behavioural changes among the customers during COVID-19 pandemic is to prevent social gatherings which is considered to be crucial in flattening the infection curve (CDC, 2020) and also suggested by Food Safety Authorities (FSA) to maintain a distance of at least six feet in food service outlets. Thus, such precautionary practices limited the operational capacity of restaurants thereby resulting in an evident decrease in revenue generation. The food service industry has witnessed a remarkable turn down in consumer footfall, as home dining trend increased amid the pandemic's fear. According to the rating agency Credit Rating Information Services of India Limited (CRISIL), pandemic has caused a 50 to 70 per cent fall in revenue generated during the fiscal year in the Indian FSI. The governments also recommended to maintain distance by reducing the seating capacity during dine- in services at restaurants (Kim and Lee, 2020). Large employee team, visit by domestic and international travellers, cross-contamination, and possibility of multiple pathogen delivery through surfaces, cutlery, crockery, and food are the factors that make the FSI susceptible to health crises (Leung and Lam, 2004). Lockdown and business shutdown orders from the government are other few reasons for the economic devastation of the restaurant business during this pandemic. These severe restrictions led to the immediate closure of businesses, thereby leading to loss of business worth billions of dollars' around the world (Kim et al., 2021). FSI succeeds on people's gatherings and outings. This industry was the hardest hit, as physical distancing method was implemented as one of the imperative measures to reduce the spread of COVID-19 and flatten the curve (Mehrotra, 2020). Moreover, customers did not visit immediately after the reopening of restaurants (Gursoy and Chi, 2020). The FSI faced major uncertainties in demand as the consumer avoided gathering in public places and were increasingly concerned about hygiene and safety (Ozili and Arun, 2020). As the consumers preferred to stay away from public places, dine-in restaurants were reliant on home deliveries, and takeaway orders which led to the closure of restaurants and unemployment around the world (Song et al.,2020). It has also impacted other associated industries like dairy, horticulture, food processing, logistics, and delivery partners.

Post-COVID Scenario

The key challenges encountered by FSI, according to Zeb et al. (2021), includes a large drop in sales, substantial layoffs, neutralised economic activity, and no support from the government. According to interviewees, adequate sanitisation, modifications in the seating area, changes in menus, and introducing fresh business concepts are the primary improvements required in existing businesses to encourage customers to return. The study significantly contributes to the food service industry by guiding them and suggesting a way forward to them on managing pandemic like situations. In June 2020, the Government of India, commenced the operations with certain Standard Operating Procedures (SOP). According to the standard operating procedures, employees in the facility must wear a proper face mask, hand gloves, and frequent sanitization and physical distancing is a must. Also, the customers were instructed to wear masks all the time while no customer was allowed to enter the premises without wearing a mask or having a fever. Also, only take away and home delivery was allowed until 10 August 2020. This situation led to a rapid shutdown of restaurants, small hotels, and stalls of street food vendors.

From the above section of review of literature, it was found that many studies have reviewed the impact of COVID-19 on FSI. With this research gap, the present study has analysed the real scenario of sales trend, pattern, and performance of restaurants from Coimbatore city during COVID and post COVID in 2020 and 2021.

Results

Table 1 displays the sales volume of the restaurant in percentage in comparison with the period during COVID in the year 2019 and post-COVID during 2021. It was identified that the sales volume has declined in April 2020 showing a value of minus 62.2 per cent and minus 64.5 per cent in July 2020 which were during the initial phases of lockdown in the country. During the same months of the next calendar year (CY), the restaurant has seen a rise in the sales volume showing a value of 94.2

Table 1: Comparison of Sales Volume Performed by the Outlet During COVID and Post-COVID in the City

Calendar Year (CY 2020)	*Apr'20*	*May'20*	*Jun'20*	*Jul'20*	*Aug'20*	*Sep'20*	*Oct'20*	*Nov'20*	*Dec'20*	
Sales	-62.2%	-56.4%	-49.8%	-64.5%	-42.7%	-5.8%	-10.3%	29.7%	-8.3%	
Dine-In	-0.3%	-0.4%	26.4%	24.3%	29.9%	35.6%	46.7%	47.0%	52.1%	
Take Away	20.9%	46.0%	33.0%	21.1%	21.7%	19.9%	15.5%	20.5%	16.8%	
Own Delivery	36.0%	15.1%	11.8%	10.1%	8.7%	9.0%	6.9%	7.0%	5.4%	
Aggregator Sale	43.4%	39.3%	28.8%	44.6%	39.6%	35.4%	31.0%	25.6%	25.7%	
Calendar Year (CY 2021)	*Jan'21*	*Feb'21*	*Mar'21*	*Apr'21*	*May'21*	*Jun'21*	*Jul'21*	*Aug'21*	*Sep'21*	*Oct'21*
Sales	-3.1%	-0.3%	57.9%	94.2%	-7.8%	-20.3%	111.3%	19.3%	-18.6%	1.7%
Dine-In	55.2%	57.2%	55.6%	47.2%	-0.2%	0.0%	46.4%	56.2%	50.7%	67.1%
Take Away	14.7%	14.2%	13.3%	16.9%	15.8%	22.3%	12.8%	14.3%	12.3%	8.1%
Own Delivery	6.0%	5.1%	5.8%	5.7%	22.1%	18.3%	9.4%	4.0%	8.0%	3.7%
Aggregator Sale	24.2%	23.5%	25.3%	30.2%	62.3%	59.5%	31.5%	25.4%	29.0%	21.1%

Source: Primary data

Table 2: Comparison Chart of Earnings before Interest, Taxes, Depreciation, and Amortization (EBITDA) for 2020-2021

Calendar Year (CY 2020)	*Apr'20*	*May'20*	*Jun'20*	*Jul'20*	*Aug'20*	*Sep'20*	*Oct'20*	*Nov'20*	*Dec'20*	
Store EBITDA	12.9%	14.0%	20.4%	13.8%	28.3%	30.6%	31.0%	29.3 %	27.0%	
Calendar Year (CY 2021)	*Jan'21*	*Feb'21*	*Mar'21*	*Apr'21*	*May'21*	*Jun'21*	*Jul'21*	*Aug'21*	*Sep'21*	*Oct'21*
Store EBITDA	33.1%	23.5%	27.3%	14.9%	10.9%	20.2%	29.9%	25.2%	22.1%	23.9%

Source: Primary data

per cent and 111.3 per cent in April and July 2021, respectively. During 2020, high sales volume was performed by aggregators, followed by own delivery and takeaways whereas in 2021, dine-in sales were higher followed by aggregators, take away, and own delivery.

The percentage of sales through an aggregator was high during COVID lockdown months (especially in April and July) since the movement of people was highly restricted. On the other hand, during post-COVID months when dine-in service was open, the sales volume had increased, except in May and June 2021, when the lockdown was implemented in the city. The reason for the same is that post-COVID, people wanted to have a social gathering with family and friends. Also, during 2020 and 2021, aggregators performance was significant in bringing up the sales volume of the restaurant.

From the Table 2, it is inferred that the Earnings before Interest, Taxes, Depreciation, and Amortization (EBITDA) was high during September and October 2020. In August, EBITDA was 28.3 per cent of since relaxations were given by the government during particular months in 2020 where as in 2021, the highest performance was in January and the performance declined as there was an increase in restrictions due to increase in COVID cases within the city.

Comparison chart of Time slot sales performed by the restaurant during 2020 and 2021 was displayed in Table 3. It is inferred from the table that, the sales volume during lunch was higher when compared to dinner during both 2020 and 2021 since time restrictions for the movement of people after 17 hours was implemented in the city during peak COVID and post-COVID months.

Table 4 displays the product-wise sales performance during 2020 and 2021. Mutton Biriyani being the favourite dish of Coimbatoreans scored the highest selling dish, varying from 27.3 per cent to 37 per cent in 2020 and 26 per cent to 29.1 per cent in 2021. Second highest selling dish from the restaurant was chicken biriyani followed by other biriyani varieties like (vegetable, mushroom, Fish, Prawn, etc.) and other dishes from the restaurant.

From Table 5, it can be observed that the sales performance on Sunday was higher when compared to other days of the week in 2020 and 2021. This is due to the fact that Sunday is holiday for most of the organisations and customers also get time to spend with their families and friends in a social gathering. Wednesday was the second highest selling during 2020 and Saturday was the second highest selling day during 2021. In 2020 and

Table 3: Comparison Chart of Time Slot Sales for 2020–21

Calendar Year (CY 2020)	*Apr'20*	*May'20*	*Jun'20*	*Jul'20*	*Aug'20*	*Sep'20*	*Oct'20*	*Nov'20*	*Dec'20*	
Lunch	78.2%	78.8%	74.0%	71.3%	76.7%	76.5%	77.0%	75.0%	76.6%	
Dinner	21.8%	21.2%	26.0%	28.7%	23.3%	23.5%	23.0%	25.0%	23.4%	
Calendar Year (CY 2021)	*Jan'21*	*Feb'21*	*Mar'21*	*Apr'21*	*May'21*	*Jun'21*	*Jul'21*	*Aug'21*	*Sep'21*	*Oct'21*
Lunch	77.1%	74.5%	74.8%	77.7%	79.9%	79.3%	84.6%	84.9%	82.8%	81.2%
Dinner	22.9%	25.5%	25.2%	22.3%	20.1%	20.7%	15.4%	15.1%	17.2%	18.8%

Source: Primary data

Table 4: Product-wise Sales Performance by the Restaurant During Calendar Year 2020–21

Calendar Year (CY 2020)	*Apr'20*	*May'20*	*Jun'20*	*Jul'20*	*Aug'20*	*Sep'20*	*Oct'20*	*Nov'20*	*Dec'20*	
Mutton Biriyani	31.1%	37.0%	33.8%	29.9%	30.5%	30.0%	27.3%	29.6%	29.8%	
Chicken Biriyani	33.2%	26.8%	21.2%	23.3%	24.0%	22.4%	20.5%	21.6%	21.7%	
Other Biriyani varieties	5.7%	5.9%	7.4%	7.6%	7.1%	7.5%	8.9%	8.8%	7.2%	
Other Dishes	25.2%	25.5%	34.1%	35.6%	35.1%	37.0%	40.8%	37.4%	39.0%	
Container Charges	4.8%	4.7%	3.5%	3.6%	3.4%	3.1%	2.6%	2.6%	2.3%	
Calendar year (CY 2021)	*Jan'21*	*Feb'21*	*Mar'21*	*Apr'21*	*May'21*	*Jun'21*	*Jul'21*	*Aug'21*	*Sep'21*	*Oct'21*
Mutton Biriyani	29.1%	28.4%	26.9%	27.0%	26.5%	26.9%	26.8%	26.8%	26.0%	26.6%
Chicken Biriyani	21.2%	20.7%	20.8%	21.8%	28.2%	31.2%	27.1%	24.2%	25.1%	23.6%
Other Biriyani varieties	8.2%	8.0%	7.9%	7.8%	6.1%	5.8%	8.5%	8.0%	7.7%	8.2%
Other Dishes	39.3%	40.8%	42.3%	40.9%	34.2%	31.3%	35.0%	38.9%	38.8%	39.9%
Container Charges	2.2%	2.1%	2.2%	2.6%	4.9%	4.9%	2.6%	2.1%	2.4%	1.6%

Source: Primary data

Table 5: Day-wise Sales Performance by the Restaurant During the Calendar Year 2020–21

Calendar Year (CY 2020)	*Apr'20*	*May'20*	*Jun'20*	*Jul'20*	*Aug'20*	*Sep'20*	*Oct'20*	*Nov'20*	*Dec'20*	
Monday	8.8%	12.6%	11.5%	11.5%	16.2%	10.3%	9.9%	11.4%	7.8%	
Tuesday	10.9%	11.4%	12.2%	13.0%	11.5%	12.5%	9.4%	8.3%	10.5%	
Wednesday	15.0%	11.1%	12.3%	22.9%	17.5%	18.3%	13.2%	12.0%	15.1%	
Thursday	14.5%	9.9%	10.6%	14.1%	14.5%	9.7%	12.5%	9.8%	13.6%	
Friday	12.0%	13.1%	10.5%	18.1%	12.5%	9.7%	14.2%	10.6%	14.2%	
Saturday	12.0%	12.5%	13.5%	20.4%	27.9%	14.4%	18.0%	19.1%	14.0%	
Sunday	26.9%	29.4%	29.6%	0.0%	0.0%	25.0%	22.8%	28.8%	24.8%	
Calendar Year (CY 2021)	*Jan'21*	*Feb'21*	*Mar'21*	*Apr'21*	*May'21*	*Jun'21*	*Jul'21*	*Aug'21*	*Sep'21*	*Oct'21*
Monday	7.6%	9.3%	11.4%	8.8%	9.8%	7.8%	8.2%	13.9%	9.8%	8.6%
Tuesday	9.4%	9.0%	11.8%	10.8%	8.7%	11.7%	9.2%	15.1%	9.6%	10.3%
Wednesday	10.4%	13.5%	15.4%	12.4%	12.2%	17.5%	13.6%	14.0%	18.0%	9.3%
Thursday	9.9%	10.3%	8.8%	13.9%	9.6%	9.6%	11.6%	11.8%	17.1%	10.5%
Friday	16.6%	10.0%	9.9%	14.4%	12.8%	11.2%	10.9%	12.2%	12.8%	12.1%
Saturday	17.7%	17.8%	15.3%	15.0%	17.5%	13.6%	19.7%	23.1%	15.7%	19.8%
Sunday	28.3%	30.0%	27.4%	24.7%	29.3%	28.6%	26.9%	9.9%	17.0%	29.5%

Source: Primary data

2021, Monday and Tuesday were the lowest selling days as they are the commencing days of the week and customers may not find time to spend at restaurant with family and friends.

Suggestions

The food service industry was very badly hit during the COVID-19 pandemic even though it is a fundamental requirement for human life. Customers generally wanted to spend their time with family and friends in a places like restaurant with good ambience, food quality, quantity, taste, reasonable cost and hospitality of employees. But after the pandemic, customers have become conscious regarding the hygiene and safety during the entire food service delivery process starting from preparation to billing of services provided by restaurants. Ministry of family and health welfare suggested SOP to be followed to contain the spread of virus through restaurant industry which includes social distancing, sanitizing, washing hands on regular intervals, wearing mask, etc., when the government of India lifted curfew in states where the infection rate decreased. Apart from SOP, restaurants can adopt the help of technology, where customer can complete the whole process from menu order to payment of services using their mobile phones (contactless menu order, servicing and billing procedures using drones, covered food service, or robot service) which may help the restaurant to bring their customers back for dine-in facility without lack of confidence in safety and hygiene at restaurants. This may also help in improving dinner time slot sales at the restaurant. When compared with second half of the week, first half of the week shows low performance in sales. To increase the sales volume in the first half of a week, more offers on dishes (5+1 offers, prize offers, offers on billing values, vouchers with offers that motivate to revisit) may be provided, that may motivate customers to engage themselves in social gathering during week days rather than week-ends.

Future Scope of the Study

The findings of the present study were focused on an organised restaurant chain located in the heart of the city. Hence the future researchers can focus the effect of COVID on unorganised restaurant chains, different restaurant types (continental, multi-cuisine, traditional cuisine, etc.), locality of the restaurant (urban, suburban, outskirts, town, etc.) or cities from different parts of India.

Conclusion

There is no doubt that FSI was hit badly during the COVID-19 pandemic but restaurants tried their level best to run the business and achieve success with trending initiatives to reach out to customers. It has become essential to operate the restaurants with SOP which has become the new normal as customers fear of getting infected from sources like restaurant industry. Hence, the study has highlighted on some factors that contribute to the sales performance during COVID and post COVID months. The present study may also help the restaurant organisations to frame strategies based on the suggestions provided to manage the sales performance in hospitality sector in adverse pandemic like situations.

References

[1] A. Bartik, Z. Cullen, M. Bertrand, E.L. Glaeser, M. Luca, and C. Stanton, (2020). 'National Bureau of Economic Research, How are Small Businesses Adjusting to COVID-19?' *Early Evidence from a Survey* (NBER Working Paper No. 26989).

[2] A. Mehrotra (2020). The Indian Restaurant Industry will Never be the Same. Available at: https://cio.economictimes.indiatimes.com/news/corporate-news/the-indian-restaurant-industry-will-never-be-the-same/75157663. Accessed on 19 November 2021.

[3] B. Santich (2004). 'The Study of Gastronomy and its Relevance to Hospitality Education and Training'. *International Journal of Hospitality Management*, 23, pp. 15–24.

[4] Centers for Disease Control and Prevention (2020). Cases in the U.S. Retrieved from https://www.nytimes.com/interactive/2021/us/covid-cases.html accessed on 02 December 2021.

[5] C. Gu and Y.J. Kim (2002). 'Penalized Likelihood Regression: General Formulation and Efficient Approximation'. *Canadian Journal of Statistics*, 30(4), pp. 619-628.

[6] C.R.D.A. Meneguel, L. Mundet, and S. Aulet (2019). 'The Role of a High-Quality Restaurant in Stimulating the Creation and Development of Gastronomy Tourism'. *International Journal of Hospitality Management*, 83, pp. 220–228.

[7] D. Gursoy and C.G. Chi (2020). 'Effects of COVID-19 Pandemic on Hospitality Industry: Review of the Current Situations and a Research Agenda'. *Journal of Hospitality Marketing and Management*, 29(5), pp. 527–529.

[8] H.G. Parsa, and A.J. Gregory (2020). Why Do Restaurants Fail? Part III: An Analysis of Macro and Micro Factors. FL, USA: The Dick Pope Sr. Institute for Tourism Studies: Winter Haven, pp. 20–28.

[9] H.G. Parsa, J.T. Self, S. Sydnor-Busso, and H.J. Yoon (2011). 'Why Restaurants Fail? Part II—The Impact of Affiliation, Location, and Size on Restaurant Failures: Results from a Survival Analysis'. *Journal of Food Service Business and Research*, 14, pp. 360–379.

[10] H.J. Song, J. Yeon, and S. Lee (2020). 'Impact of the COVID-19 Pandemic: Evidence from the US Restaurant Industry'. *International Journal of Hospitality Management*, 92, pp. 1–7.

[11] J. Kim, J. Jun, L.R. Tang, and T. Zheng (2018). 'The Behavioral and Intermediate Effects of Advertising on Firm Performance: An Empirical Investigation of the Restaurant Industry'. *Journal Hospitality and Tourism Research*, 42, pp. 319–337.

[12] J. Kim, J. Kim, S.K. Lee and L.R. Tang (2020). 'Effects of Epidemic Disease Outbreaks on Financial Performance of Restaurants: Event Study Method Approach'. *Journal Hospitality and Tourism Management*, 43, pp. 32–41.

[13] K. Severson, and D. Yaffe-Bellany (20 March 2020). 'Independent restaurants brace for the unknown'. *The New York Times* available at https://www.nytimes.com/2020/03/20/dining/local-restaurants-coronavirus.html. (Cross reference) accessed on 25 November 2021.

[14] M.d. M. Alonso-Almeida, K Bremser, and J. Llach (2015). 'Proactive and Reactive Strategies Deployed by Restaurants in Times of Crisis: Effects on Capabilities, organisation and Competitive Advantage'. *International Journal of Contemporary Hospitality Management*, 27, pp. 1641–1661.

[15] M. MacDonald, R. Piazza, and G. Sher (2020). 'A Simple Guide to Estimating the Impact of COVID-19 on Travel and Hospitality Activity', *IMF – Special Series on COVID-19*, pp. 1–10.

[16] M. Sigala, (2020). 'Tourism and COVID-19: Impacts and Implications for Advancing and Resetting Industry and Research. *Journal of Business Research*, 117, pp. 312–321.

[17] P. Leung, and T. Lam, (2004). 'Crisis Management During the SARS Threat: A Case Study of the Metropole Hotel in Hong Kong'. *Journal of Human Resource of Hospitality and Tourism*, 3(1), pp. 47–57.

[18] P.K. Ozili, and T. Arun (2020). Spillover of COVID-19: Impact on the Global Economy, p. 27. Available at SSRN: https://ssrn.com/abstract=3562570 or http://dx.doi.org/10.2139/ssrn.3562570

[19] P. Pressman, A.S. Naidu, and R. Clemens, (2020). 'COVID-19 and Food Safety: Risk Management and Future Considerations'. *Nutrition Today*, 55(3), pp.125–128.

[20] R. Kalaivani, and P. Girija (2018). 'A Study on Consumer Perception and Satisfaction Towards Restaurants with Reference to Coimbatore City'. *Journal of Emerging Technologies and Innovative Research*, 5(6), pp. 421-434.

[21] S. Jung, and S. Jang (2019). 'To Cluster or Not to Cluster?: Understanding Geographic Clustering by Restaurant Segment'. *International Journal of Hospitality Management*, 77, pp. 448–457.

[22] S. Vig, and R. N Agarwal (2021). 'Repercussions of COVID-19 on Small Restaurant Entrepreneurs: The Indian context'. *Strategic Change*, 30(2), pp. 145–152.

[23] S. Zeb, S.S. Hussain, and A. Javed, and Y.C Jim Wu (Reviewing editor) (2021). 'COVID-19 and A Way Forward for Restaurants and Street Food Vendors', *Cogent Business & Management*, 8(1), p. 10.

[24] T. Baum, and N.T.T. Hai (2020). 'Hospitality, Tourism, Human Rights and the Impact of COVID'. *International Journal of Contemporary Hospitality Management*, 32 (7). pp. 2397–2407.

[25] T.J. Haas (2008). Today's Foodservice Industry Demands Strong Leadership: Business Publications.

[26] T. Watanabe, and Y. Omori (2020). 'How Much Did People Refrain from Service Consumption Due to the Outbreak of COVID-19?', Center for Advanced Research in Finance, Faculty of Economics, The University of Tokyo CARF F-Series; p. 477.

[27] W. Ding, R. Levine, C., Linand, W. Xie (2020). *Corporate Immunity to the COVID-19 Pandemic. Working Paper 27055*, Massachusetts: National Bureau of Economic Research.

[28] Y. Wang (2009). 'The Impact of Crisis Events and Macroeconomic Activity on Taiwan's International Inbound Tourism Demand'. *Tourism Management*, 30, pp. 75–82.

[29] Y. Yang, H. Liu, and X. Chen (2020). 'COVID-19 and Restaurant Demand: Early Effects of the Pandemic and Stay-at-Home orders'. *International Journal of Contemporary Hospitality Management*, 13(12), pp. 3809–3834.

[30] Zomato (2020). 'State of the Restaurant Industry in India'. Available at omato.com/blog/wp-content/uploads/2020/08/Indian-Restaurant-Industry-—-Mid-COVID-19-Report.pdf. Accessed on 01 December 2021.

Websites

[1] Retrieved from Statista Research Department (2021). Available at https://www.statista.com/statistics/1104835/coronavirus-travel-tourism-employment-loss/ accessed on 02 December, 2021.

[2] Retrieved from WHO (2020). Retrieved from https://www.who.int/news/item/29-06-2020-covidtimeline accessed on 02 December, 2021.

CHAPTER 9

Determinants of the Emerging Paradigms in Helping Professions: Lessons from Pandemics, Climate Change and Growing Inequality

SIGAMANI PANNEER[1], F.X. LOVELINA LITTLE FLOWER[2], HILARIA SOUNDARI M.[3], LEKHA BHAT[4], TRESA SUGIRTHA[5], SANTHOSH J.S.[6], MICHELLE ELIZABETH MATHEW[7] AND MHADENO Y. HUMTSOE[8]

Abstract: *The socio-economic and cultural determinants of health and health systems across the globe are challenged swiftly by the COVID-19 pandemic, witnessing humanitarian crisis in many parts of the world. The situation calls for effective learning and practical action on the associated link between health, climate change, and growing inequality. Analysing the keynote presentations of the eminent speakers invited from United Kingdom (UK), Japan, Australia, Germany, South Africa, Afghanistan, and India for an International Virtual Symposium titled, 'Pandemics, Climate Change and Growing Inequality: Emerging Paradigm Shift in*

[1] Professor and Head, The School of Social Sciences and Humanities, The Department of Social Work, Central University of Tamil Nadu, Thiruvarur, India. E-mail: sigamanip@cutn.ac.in

[2] Professor and Head, The Department of Social Work, Bharathiar University, Coimbatore. E-mail: lovelinabu@gmail.com

[3] Assistant Professor, The Centre for Applied Research, Gandhigram Rural Institute, Gandhigram. E-mail: hilariasoundari@gmail.com

[4] Assistant Professor, The Department of Epidemiology and Public Health, Central University of Tamil Nadu, Thiruvarur. E-mail: lekhabhatd@gmail.com

[5] Assistant Professor, The Department of Social Work, PSG College of Arts and Science, Coimbatore. E-mail: tresaprem@yahoo.com

[6] Senior Research Scholar (UGC-NET), The Department of Social Work, Bharathiar University, Coimbatore. E-mail: jssantoshmail@gmail.com

[7] Senior Research Scholar (UGC-NET), The Department of Social Work, Bharathiar University, Coimbatore. Email: michssearch@gmail.com

[8] Ph.D. Scholar, The Centre for Applied Research, Gandhigram Rural Institute, Gandhigram. E-mail: mhadenohumtsoe91@gmail.com

Helping Professions', the article explores social pandemics, COVID-19 lockdown's effects and responses, crises preparedness and management, community based actions as the influential factors that determine the emerging paradigms in social work and public health. Technological innovation, climate change adversities, and the scope of helping professions are briefed. This paper identifies thrust areas for future direction of research, professional practice, and shares key learning and recommendations. Recognising the need for transdisciplinary research projects, the symposium invites academia and health practitioners across the continents for dissemination of holistic knowledge and cross-learning strategies in managing crises situations.

Keywords: COVID-19, Pandemics, Climate Change, Growing Inequality, Social Work, Public Health, Transdisciplinary Research

Introduction

As the world today is witnessing the effects of pandemic, climate change, and growing inequalities, the World Bank estimates around 11 million people will be pushed into poverty due to COVID-19 pandemic and the International Monetary Fund (IMF) preliminary estimates the economic-impact of the pandemic is around 2 trillion US dollars (USD). To end the pandemic, United Nations (UN) was immediate to health response for controlling the spread of the novel coronavirus and focus on people especially, women, low-wage workers, youth, informal sector and risk-prone vulnerable groups. International Labour Organisation (ILO) estimates 25 million people are on the verge of losing their jobs, especially informal sector to be worst hit due to lack of social protection. The United Nations Educational, Scientific and Cultural Organisation (UNESCO) estimates 1.25 billion students are affected and reaching goal 4 of the Sustainable Development Goals (SDGs) has become a serious challenge in attaining quality education.

The COVID-19 pandemic has widened the scope of helping professions, calls for reflection and proactive action to tackle the humanitarian crisis and disaster. Disasters often can lead to increase in gender-based violence such as domestic violence and social work has a critical role in empowering and facilitating safety of women and children (O'Leary and Tsui, 2020). While governments are doing their best to handle the crisis situation with lock-down measures however, the lopsided process is causing more problems particularly to the vulnerable groups. The sheltering-in-place and stay-at-home orders have affected many older adults as they have lost their usual ways to connect with support networks as well as health and social service providers and are spending increased time alone (Berg-Weger and Morley, 2020). In this tough context, the social workers should reconsider the person-in-the-environment as a complex and critical emerging domain of Social Work theories and practice, a domain where gender awareness is fundamental (Margaret, 2013).

The effects of climate change are becoming increasingly relevant to the social work profession and specific groups such as women are at risk of further disadvantage unless collective action is taken to circumvent the impact of climate change (Heather and Jennifer, 2013). Climate change will also affect the ability of individuals to use food effectively by altering the conditions for food safety and changing the disease pressure from vector, water, and food-borne diseases (Josef and Francesco, 2007). While India is a fast developing economy in the world, it is also one of the most unequal countries. Access to health and health care needs is an incessant problem and many Indians are pushed into poverty because of healthcare costs every year. Similarly, the reality of gender inequality in India is very complex and diversified because it exists in every field like education, employment opportunities, health, cultural issues, social issues, economic issues, etc. (Jha and Nagar, 2015). Hence, it becomes imperative to understand various economic, political and psycho-social impacts of the pandemic, climate change, and growing inequality and need to devise a holistic research approach through transdisciplinary collaboration in the development of pandemic plans not only mean more robust research but will have a long-term influence on the formulation of influenza pandemic preparedness policy (Mamelund, 2017). Developing professional capacity among the public health workforce (a diverse group of professionals), for evidence based decision making through training, has the potential to decrease disease burden in the population (Jacob et al., 2018). The ongoing and future social science research findings must support and facilitate a vision beyond crisis and transfer fear, sorrow, and loss into empowerment and social transformation.

Background and Objectives

The COVID-19 pandemic has exposed an increase in gender inequality, health inequities, and structural weakness of health systems in different countries. Along with these, various reports about climate change have also linked pandemics with zoonotic diseases. The Coronavirus disease (COVID-19) is considered one such zoonotic disease and more such diseases are predicted in the future. The developmental activities of social work and public health related projects addressing inequality have become a standstill during pandemic and hence calls for a reorientation of the helping professions. In this context, an active intellectual response becomes imperative to understand and act on issues related to pandemics, climate change, and growing inequalities across the globe.

The International Virtual Symposium was hosted by the Department of Social Work, Central University of Tamil Nadu (Thiruvarur), the Department of Social Work, Bharathiar University (Coimbatore), and The Centre for Applied Research, Gandhigram Rural Institute, Gandhigram (Tamil Nadu). The symposium intends to contextualise the problems of the global pandemic, explore proactive responses, identify evidence-based activities in the helping profession as well as to reflect upon the reality and come with innovative solutions which can eventually lead to future research, collaboration, and networking across the globe.

The objective of this article is: (a) to explore the determinant factors influencing the emerging paradigms in the helping professions across the globe due to pandemics, climate change, and growing inequities, (b) identify the scope of the helping professions during the crisis, and (c) present key learning and recommendations from the International Virtual symposium.

Brief Note on Keynote Speakers

Matteo Convertino, Dr. Eng PhD, is an Associate Professor in Bio-complexity, Data Science and Ecosystem Design at Hokkaido University, Japan, at the Faculty of Information Science and Technology. He directs the Nexus Lab that is focused on synthesis, predictions and design of complex multi-scale ecosystems as well as development of bio-inspired technology.

Nonie Harris, PhD, is an Associate Professor at College of Arts, Society, and Education, James Cook University, Australia. Nonie's research and publications have focused on feminist methodologies, feminist theory, work integrated learning, teaching research, and child care policy in cross national contexts. Currently, she is a member of the management committee of the North Queensland Domestic Violence Resource Service.

Nevashnee Perumal, PhD, is a lecturer in the Department of Social Development Professions, Nelson Mandela University, South Africa. She is a qualified, registered social work practitioner and published her works in the field such as elderly care, family therapy, child protection and family welfare services, social work management and leadership. She is currently devoting her research energies into de-colonial social work in higher education.

Dr. Gerhard Rott, PhD, Social Work Professional and Head of the Department for International Relations, Diocese of Eichstätt-Germany. He has published his work in leading journals and has visited India (Manipal, Chennai, Cochin) to deliver lectures on political education in the context of International Social Work, visited Lithuania (Kansas) to talk on development cooperation as a factor of prevention of migration, and Colombia (Medellin) to talk on challenges and perspectives for the International social work- management.

Komali Kantamaneni, PhD, is a coastal scientist at Warsash School of Maritime Science and Engineering, Solent University, United Kingdom. Her research focuses mainly on coastal vulnerability, natural disasters, natural hazards, climate change, water infrastructure, and Geographic Information System (GIS) mapping. Her research on 'Assessing coastal vulnerability: development of a combined physical and economic index' produced for the first time a combined vulnerability assessment based on physical science parameters and economic drivers.

Mohammad Qaseem Haidari, PhD, is a Deputy Minister for Policy, Coordination and Planning, State Ministry for Disaster Management and Humanitarian Affairs, Afghanistan. He has 10 years of senior leadership experience in coordination, management, and evaluation of humanitarian and social development programmes in post-conflict areas. He has expertise in coordinating mainstreaming humanitarian assistance into multi-input area development initiatives, engaging in diplomatic affairs as well as donor coordination with heads of donor agencies and government.

Sigamani Panneer PhD, is a Professor and Head, the Department of Social Work, School of Social Sciences and Humanities, Central University of Tamil Nadu, India. A recipient of prestigious Raman fellowship, he served as visiting Professor at the School of Public Health, University of Minnesota (USA), Tianjin University of Finance and Economics (China), and Jishou University (China). He has authored articles of national and international repute published by Palgrave, Macmillan, Sage, Springer,

Wiley, Elsevier, BioMed Central, Economic and Political Weekly, and Bloomsbury.

Lekha Bhat, PhD, is an Assistant Professor at the Department of Epidemiology and Public Health, Central University of Tamil Nadu, India. She has basic training in Public Health with an MPhil and a PhD in social medicine and community health from Jawaharlal Nehru University (JNU), New Delhi. She has published papers with reputed journals in Springer, Wiley, and Bloomsbury.

Key Factors Influencing the Paradigm Shift in the Helping Profession

The experiences, views, and opinions of the keynote speakers presented in the virtual symposium on pandemics, climate change, and growing

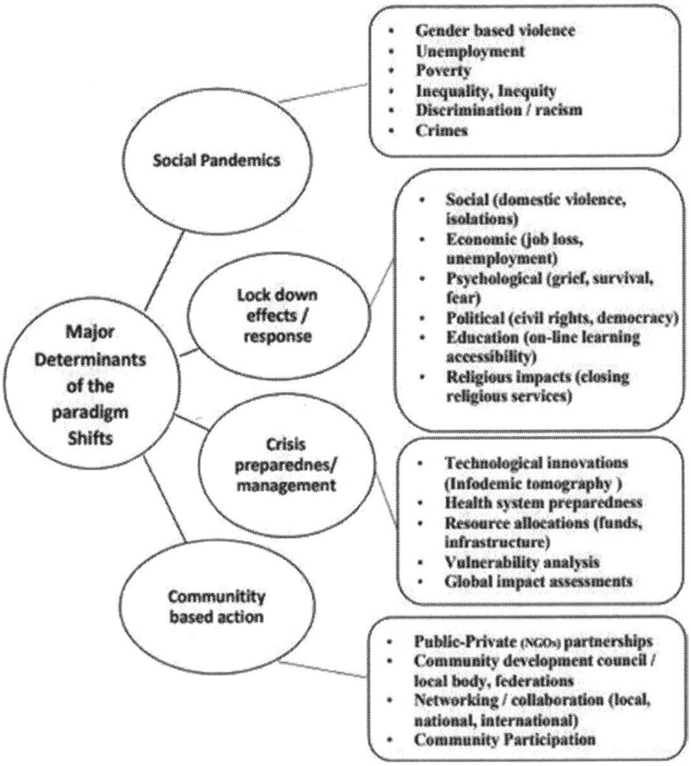

Figure 1: Determinants/Key Factors Influencing the Paradigm Shift in the Helping Professions

Source: International Virtual Symposium on Pandemics, Climate Change and Growing Inequality: The emerging paradigm shift in helping profession (Sigamani P et al., 2020)

inequality were analysed and major determinants of the emerging paradigms in the helping professions are identified and mapped as shown in the Figure 1.

Social Pandemics: Issues and Challenges

Dr. Nevashnee presented on 'Social Work in South Africa and Pandemics: Lessons from African Wisdom' and examined the pandemic in social dimensions, raising consciousness about the need for building human solidarity against pandemics. She challenged to look into the word 'pandemic' beyond its medical meaning to a much broader societal realm and recognize 'social pandemics' that exists in the form of poverty, unemployment, inequity, racism, white domination, crimes, gender based violence, and inequality considering the suffering of the people in growing unequal conditions.

Reflecting on 'Gender and COVID-19 in Australia', Dr. Nonie Harris said that the Australian Government's Workplace Gender Equality Agency (WGEA) used gender lens to focus on women during the pandemic. She noted that the effects on women includes their predominant employment in the healthcare sector, responsibility for care work, gendered division of domestic duties, financial security, and domestic violence (WGEA, 2020). The Australian Institute of Criminology reported that for many women, the pandemic coincided with the onset or escalation of violence and abuse. Dr. Harris commented on fee hike in social work education by the Australian government and observed that since many students are mature-aged women and first generation university students, social work education potentially leads to a lasting and positive change in their life circumstance and so an attack on social work education is, in many ways, an attack on women's opportunities. In her view, the global pandemic has not slowed the conservative agendas rather created a 'covid cloak' where women's disadvantages are further entrenched. She opined that COVID-19 has brought clarity and impact on neo-liberal social policies on the marginalized, particularly on women.

Dr. Gerald shared his views on the German media focusing its news and statistics more on Latin America and Asia but not on Africa which shows the negligence and discriminatory attitudes that are being evident. Mentioning that the senior citizens have become vulnerable to psychological problems since they are unable to meet their children and grandchildren, Dr. Gerhard said the meetings and choirs are held in the courtyards to handle the isolation, where the children of the elderly greet them from outside. People in special homes (for mental illness and with other problems) do equally suffer and the problem remains uncertain in dealing with these challenges. The counsellors were given permission with special orders for counselling sessions to serve the people in need.

Dr. Lekha opined that humanitarian crisis witnessed by today's society in terms of poverty, inequity, regional conflicts, civil wars, and disasters are to be explored and discussion should be made on how COVID-19 has impacted global economy, loss of jobs, changes in migrants' lives, gender violence, and increased burden on women while resulting in health inequity. 'Gender issues (dual burden on work, and limits of work from home), domestic violence (violation of human rights) and people with special needs including elderly (social security, lack of access to essential services) are the problems during the pandemic crisis', said Dr. Sigamani while identifying the thrust areas of research like advocating priority based social welfare services supporting women, mobilizing women's leadership with doable strategies, elderly, and people with special needs.

The Lockdown Effects and Response

Sharing the experiences in South Africa, Dr. Nevashnee, opined that lockdown was good as it reduced the spread of COVID-19 and it was bad as it caused many to lose livelihoods, increased poverty, and domestic violence. It was unjust due to military and police brutality, corruptions, undignified conditions in hospitals, and online teaching/learning became unreachable for the poor and marginalised.

Due to the COVID-19 situation, throughout the globe, in spite of countries facing challenges and troubles to lift its citizens from economic despair, some countries did managed to give relief to its citizens by rolling out special economic packages to its citizens to meet their basic needs. Dr. Gerhard shared that in Germany during lockdown, the government extended monetary support to the private firms to assure its employees their monthly income and are paid initially up to 67 per cent, gradually increasing to 77 per cent after 4 months and further up to 87 per cent after 8 months. Dr. Gerhard also shared that the policy in Germany allows parents, either father or mother, to avail paid leaves for 15 days to stay at home and take care of their unwell kids.

Dr. Lekha viewed that restrictions on economic activities resulted in high economic and social cost due to lockdown and quarantine. More than 30 million people could fall into poverty in the absence of active policies to protect or substitute income flows to vulnerable populations (UNDP, 2020) apart from impacting their health and well-being.

Dr. Sigamani highlighted the problems during the pandemic crisis which includes, (a) psychological impact (suicide, grief, survival, fear), (b) economic impact (plight of informal sector, job loss, pay cut, lack of data/information), (c) political impacts (ideological differences, lack of need based initiatives, geo-political cooperation, civil rights, and democracy), (d) educational impact (closure of educational institutions), (e) individual isolation (lack of human happiness and well-being), and (f) religious impact (closure and cancellation of religious services).

Crisis Preparedness and Management

Dr. Lekha noted that climate change has resulted an increase in the occurrences of various zoonotic diseases due to anthropogenic activities. Moreover, the International Panel on Climate Change (2020) warns about the link between climate change, food basket shrinking, and zoonotic diseases.

On presenting the coastal landslide hazards and risk management, Dr. Komali shared a case study done in the UK that systematically analysed the landslides in the UK from 2000 to 2016 (except Northern Ireland) by employing a two-path methodology in understanding the coastal landslide risk and management. Path I is the analysis of coastal landslides while Path II is opinion gleaned from experts all over the world on prediction of coastal landslides and generating GIS map based on the data. The study revealed that out of the 966 landslides (2000-16), 749 were coastal landslides and 24 per cent of the coastal landslides were reported from urban areas. England accounts for 68 per cent of the total landslides followed by Scotland with 21 per cent and the rest 11 per cent has occurred in Wales. The recommendations given to the policy makers in the UK are: (a) early warning system for landslide risks is necessary, (b) England is highly prone to landslides and needs immediate attention, especially the southern coastal parts, and (c) more fund has to be allocated to encourage landslide related research activities which will lead to better strategies and policies to reduce the risks of landslides. Dr. Komali mentioned that in some coastal areas, houses are very near to the coast and its residents are not ready to move outside due to their emotional attachment to their places. While all the mitigation measures are implemented by the UK government, certain coastlines are managed by private companies.

Dr. Haidari said that due to climate change, Afghanistan being an agrarian community, suffered from a severe drought having tremendous impact on livelihoods and thereby interrupted the support system of the local community. He added, the recent flash floods in the year 2020, have destroyed peoples' shelters in most places and these challenges have led to the low availability of humanitarian workers on the ground in times of COVID-19. Dr. Haidari sees preparation as an important key segment for humanitarian response. He presented the government's responses in Afghanistan and community participation in disaster management, stating that arm conflicts, limited social protection system, inadequate health care capacity, and insufficient preparedness made Afghanistan face initial difficulty in identifying, testing, and tracking new cases of COVID-19. Dr. Haidari viewed that even though the healthcare system has improved over the past 17 years, the government still faces challenges for promoting functional responses to COVID-19. Testing facilities, isolation, and hospitalisation are increasing and provided on daily basis by both public and private hospitals. He noted there is a lack of awareness among the rural public about the pandemic and the Afghan government is trying to reach them through its disaster response team.

Dr. Gerhard appreciated the efforts of the German government for doing tremendous job in dealing with the pandemic and preventing huge spread among its population.

Dr Matteo presented on the Infodemic Tomography (InTo), a predictive model of socio-epidemiological patterns of COVID-19, by using a specific social media data (twitter tweets) over a preferred geospatial and temporal area. The model analysed tweet sentiments that reveals behavioural dynamics for meaningful risk perceptions and predictability of new cases and hospitalization in a particular geographical area. The tweets were classified under eight themes: (1) case identification, contact tracing, and related measures, (2) environmental measures, (3) healthcare and public health capacity, (4) resource allocation, (5) risk communication, (6) social distancing, (7) travel restriction, and (8) returning to normal life. Tweet dynamics, with regard to positive sentiments, was used to predict pattern of hospitalisation and cases over space every week. Higher the positivity, lower the hospitalisation. The model helps in understanding the healthcare pressure (HP), the ability of healthcare system in terms of its infrastructure and treatment capacities. Dr. Matteo said that the model is validated by calculating the risk, gap and divergence indices over a period of time by considering the new cases, hospitalisation and the difference between the prediction and observation. Higher the divergence between positivity and hospitalisation, lower the predictability in short term (depending on data availability). The model uses the linear correlation coefficient in the geokriging for a weekly update on the relationship between positivity and hospitalisation.

In propounding the prospective areas of research, Dr. Sigamani adds:

(a) identifying easily available, accessible, affordable, and culturally adoptable local technology;
(b) develop capabilities at all levels for emergency, pandemic prevention, and management;
(c) reactive state leadership, and
(d) identify best practices and adopt doable strategies for crisis mitigation.

Community Based Actions

Dr. Harris quoted the remarks made by Dr. Cassandra Goldie, CEO of the Australian Council of Social Service (ACOSS) that, 'during this crisis, many people have reached out to community service charities for support, including food relief, mental health, domestic violence, and financial counselling services'. Dr. Harris opined that community based action is sufficient to challenge and change the government's mind and cited how the pressure from social work community made the Australian government withdraw from its decision of exorbitant hiking of social work education fees.

Dr. Haidari said that the government of Afghanistan, in partnership with the private sector, distributes food to the beneficiaries who are selected through the local body (council) besides giving the community face masks and sanitizers. During humanity crises compounded with COVID-19, Afghanistan requires humanitarian support for 9.5 million people in 2020 as reported by the United Nations Development Programme (UNDP), Afghanistan. Afghanistan faces huge challenge of humanitarian crises during COVID-19 and community participation is the key for the disaster management system to engage with organisations and communities through its Community Development Council (CDC).

Dr. Sigamani identifies the thrust areas of research that includes:

(a) government response in planning and response, ensuring the community participation especially the vulnerable population including informal sector;

(b) organising communities to ensure alternative livelihood opportunities along with availability ofhealthcare and essential services, community participation, and accountability;
(c) strengthen inter-organisational coordination, and
(d) local responsibility with centre's coordination.

Dr. Sigamani said that strengthening community based crisis risk management and replicating best practices from field learnings are the expected outcome of the proposed projects that is to be raised up from this Virtual International Symposium.

Scope of the Helping Professions during the crisis

Dr. Nevashnee said that the scope of social work during the medical pandemic includes:

(a) community education on prevention of virus transmission;
(b) researching community strengths, capabilities, and structural supports required to deal with medical pandemic on top of societal pandemics
(c) trauma debriefing to frontline medical personnel; and
(d) psychosocial support for the COVID-19 victims and people facing job loss.

She opined that social workers have to reflect critically by redefining roles, recognising the need for solidarity among social work professionals and take ownership of the spaces by forming or joining an action network, by inviting government officials into the discussion, by publishing statements of support or dissent and growing the public dialogue. Dr. Nevashnee said that the South African government has taken no effort to collaborate with social workers to deal with the social effects of the pandemic as any welfare measure is hindered by corruption and inefficiency and has led to the growing divide between government and community-based organisations.

Dr. Gerhard raised the cause of concern in Germany during lockdown as social workers were not able to meet and interact with the children from marginalised or migrant communities and the situation pushed the social workers to attend virtual meetings in digital platforms with their organisations and clients for planning and executing the next. The helping professionals should explore, learn, and make use of technologies in meeting the needs and demands of the profession which could help during crisis situations.

Exploring why social work and public health matters for international development, Dr. Lekha stressed on problems and questions like response of the helping professions during the crisis by finding alternative and holistic solutions, solving complex problems while remaining committed to sustainable development models. Dr. Sigamani proposed that book proposal on the International Virtual Symposium theme, looks for content that are broadly inter-disciplinary and trans-disciplinary to understand relevance of social work and public health practice methods and crisis response.

Key Learnings and Recommendations

The recommendations put-forward from key learnings after synthesising the presentations from the experts are:

(a) to understand healthcare pressure on health systems, technical data through emerging models like infodemic tomography can be used to predict the epidemiological pattern, social, and behavioural dynamics, by studying social media tweets over a particular time, and space to arrive at meaningful risk perceptions and predictability of new cases and hospitalisation;

(b) 'social pandemics' is alarming everywhere in the globe, which has widened the role of the helping professions to devise community-based actions at all levels, initiating dialogues between the community, government and with various stakeholders for successful implementation of social welfare policies, and disaster managements strategies;

(c) legislators, political parties to work together beyond their political and other differences to help people especially, the vulnerable populations of the country to overcome the crisis situation;

(d) researching community strengths, capabilities, and structural supports required for dealing with medical, and social pandemics;

(e) understanding the needs that includes trauma debriefing of frontline medical personnel dealing with terminal patients on daily death as well as compassion fatigue, extending psychosocial support to individuals and families on separation anxiety due to COVID-19, and for restoring dignity and reducing stress for people facing job loss;

(f) due to the impact of climate change around the globe in health and development, to draw future directions it is important to undertake vulnerability analysis, global impact assessment by allocating funds to encourage research activities related to landslides and other natural disasters as well as to understand and minimize the risks of landslides and other such natural disasters.

Conclusion

The International Virtual Symposium opened a space for discussion on themes related to pandemics, climate change, and growing inequality. Pandemic situation has made us to understand the weakened social security systems, welfare measures, and health systems' vulnerability across the world. On technological front, emerging models like infodemic tomography has enabled us to understand the social and behavioural dynamics which can predict the epidemiological pattern and healthcare pressure on health systems. The general consensus was sensed during the symposium for community-based actions at all levels by social workers, the liaison between the community and government and thereby, encouraging community participation. The symposium stressed the necessity of researching community strengths, capabilities, and structural supports required to deal with medical and societal pandemics while protecting the front line workers' health and extending psychosocial support to the victim and families affected by COVID-19 pandemic. To understand and explore the paradigm shifts in helping professions, it is important to identify the relevance of social work, public health practices, methods, and crisis response, undertake trans and inter-disciplinary approaches of research, recognize best practices including failures, policy relevance, and evidence based policies, build networking and collaborations, set development indicators, and devise crisis management strategies.

Acknowledgements

Foremost gratitude to the Vice Chancellors of the hosting Universities, Professor R. Karpaga Kumaravel (PhD), Vice Chancellor (Acting), Central University of Tamil Nadu (Thiruvarur), Professor P. Kaliraj (PhD), Vice Chancellor, Bharathiar University (Coimbatore), and Professor B. Subburaj (PhD), Vice Chancellor i/c, Gandhigram Rural Institute (Gandhigram) for their immense support and encouragement towards this joint initiative. To all the keynote speakers for sharing their experiential knowledge. Thanks to Dr. R. Balu Ramu for his technical assistance towards successful conduction of the International Virtual symposium.

References

[1] H. Boetto and J. McKinnon (2013). 'Rural Women and Climate Change: A Gender Inclusive Perspective', *Australian Social Work*, 66:2, pp. 234-47.

[2] J. Schmidhuber and F.N. Tubiello (2007). 'Global Food Security Under Climate Change', *Proceedings of the National Academy of Sciences*, December 2007, 104 (50), pp. 19703–708.

[3] M. Alston (2013), 'Environmental Social Work: Accounting for Gender in Climate Disasters', *Australian Social Work*, 66:2, pp. 218–33.

[4] M. Berg-Weger and J.E. Morley (2020). Editorial: Loneliness and Social Isolation in Older adults during the COVID-19 pandemic: Implications for Gerontological Social Work. *The Journal of Nutrition, Health & Aging*, 24(5), pp. 456–458.

[5] P. Jha and N. Nagar (2015). 'A Study of Gender Inequality in India', *The International Journal of Indian Psychology*, 2(3), pp. 46–53.

[6] P. O'Leary and M.S. Tsui (2020). 'Ten Gentle Reminders to Social Workers in the Pandemic', *International Social Work*, 63(3), pp. 273–74.

[7] P. Sigamani, F.X. Lovelina Little Flower, M. Hilari Soundari, Lakha Bhatt, J. Tresa Sugirtha, J.S. Santhosh, Michelle Elizabeth Mathew (2020). 'Pandemics, Climate Change and Growing Inequality: Emerging Paradigm Shift in Helping Professions'. Available at SSRN: https://ssrn.com/abstract=3694271

[8] R.R. Jacob, K. Duggan, P. Allen, P.C. Erwin, K. Aisaka, S.C. Yang, and R.C. Brownson (2018), 'Preparing Public Health Professionals to Make Evidence-Based Decisions: A Comparison of Training Delivery Methods in the United States', *Front. Public Health*, 6: 257.

[9] S.E. Mamelund (2017). 'Social Inequality – A Forgotten Factor in Pandemic Influenza Preparedness', *Journal of the Norwegian Medical Association*, June 2017, 137(12-13), pp. 911–13.

CHAPTER 10

Emerging Challenges in Disaster Risk Reduction in India

Sigamani Panneer[1], Santosh Kumar[2], Vigneshwaran Subbiah Akkayasamy[3], Aswathi K.R.[4] and Sunitha V.G.[5]

Abstract: *Natural disasters have become more common in recent years, emphasising the need for disaster risk management and disaster risk reduction (DRR). Disaster risks are determined by disasters and their degree of vulnerability on human groups who suffer losses as a result of the disaster. The development process has a significant impact on disaster risk. In most countries, the development process has a significant impact on disaster risk. Rebuilding from disasters will be devastating for poor countries thus, it is vital to adopt disaster management systems that include prevention, readiness, response, and recovery on one side and development activities on the other. Intergovernmental processes and partnerships are needed to meet 'Emerging Challenges for Disaster Risk Reduction'. Knowledge, evidence generation, and application are key aspects for building development resilient infrastructure. Multi-stakeholders' participation, risk data and information, good practice, policy guidance, tools, and capacity building can support in designing*

[1] Professor and Head, The School of Social Sciences and Humanities, The Department of Social Work, Central University of Tamil Nadu, Thiruvarur, India. E-mail: sigamanip@cutn.ac.in

[2] Professor & Head, Governance, Public Policy and Inclusive Disaster Risk Reduction, National Institute of Disaster Management, Delhi.
E-mail: profsantosh@gmail.com

[3] PhD Scholar, The School of Social Sciences and Humanities, The Department of Social Work, Central University of Tamil Nadu, Thiruvarur, India.
E-mail: vickyfrommadurai@gmail.com

[4] PhD Scholar, The School of Social Sciences and Humanities, The Department of Social Work, Central University of Tamil Nadu, Thiruvarur, India.
E-mail: aswathiramachand@gmail.com

[5] PhD Scholar, The School of Social Sciences and Humanities, The Department of Social Work, Central University of Tamil Nadu, Thiruvarur, India.
Email: sunitha_vg@wvi.org

constructive intervention programmes to address the needs of all sections of the community affected by the disaster. Disaster risk can be effectively addressed if age and gender-related needs are factored into situation analysis for development programme formulation. A three-day workshop organised by the Central University of Tamil Nadu, in collaboration with National Institute of Disaster Management on 'Emerging challenges for disaster risk reduction: New strategy and 15th finance commission' was held from 27 May to 29 May 2021. The first day of the training programme dealt with do's and don'ts during COVID-19. The second day of the workshop was about disaster and development resilient infrastructure, emerging challenges for DRR, and strategies to overcome emerging challenges in DRR with special reference to children. The session on 'Disaster Funding 15th Finance Commission: Public Policy for Disaster Risk Reduction' was held on the final day of the conference. The training sessions stressed the importance of multi-stakeholders' participation, risk data and information, good practice, policy guidance, tools, and capacity building that can support in designing constructive intervention programmes to address the needs of all sections of the community affected by the disaster.

Keywords: Disaster Risk Reduction, Disaster Management, Development, Emerging+67 Challenges, Multi-stakeholders

Background

Globally, disasters are becoming more frequent and severe as a result of expanding population, global climate change, earthquakes, and a rise in disease-carrying vectors, resulting in massive loss of life and property damage. As per the World Disasters Report 2016, around 7,72,000 individuals perished worldwide as a result of disasters between 2006 and 2015 (Sanderson & Sharma, 2016). Despite significant advances in technology and knowledge, including satellite surveillance, both developing and developed countries are becoming more vulnerable to natural disasters (Deken, 2007). The Spanish flu pandemic (1918–19) which killed 25 to 30 million people and the Tokyo earthquake (1923) which killed 1.5 lakh people are two notable natural disasters over the last 100 years. The China floods of 1931 killed 3.7 million people, a cyclone killed 1,40,000 people in Bangladesh in 1991, and the tsunami killed 2,30,000 people and displaced 1.7 million people across 14 nations in 2004. However, hurricane Katrina (2005) was the most expensive natural disaster in the United States, costing 1 trillion dollars in damages (Kirch, 2008). Since the 1970s, India has seen thirty big disasters.

India is vulnerable to natural calamities because of huge mountainous regions, 7,500 kilometre of coastlines, extensive deserts, woodlands, waterways, densely inhabited urban centres, and variations of hot and cold environmental areas (Kadri, 2019). The Sendai Framework for Disaster Risk Reduction (SFDRR) is a UN policy framework that strongly endorses science and technology (Aitsi-Selmi, 2016). To identify gaps, interdependencies, social difficulties, and catastrophe risks, the SFDRR encourages investment in creating innovative approaches in long-term and workable solution disaster risk management research (Izumi et al., 2019). There is a rising necessity to consider disasters in terms of development. Disasters can be catastrophic to communities and set back development efforts greatly. However, in the aftermath of a disaster, it may provide an opportunity to invest in development activities. Communities can remake themselves as a result of disasters. The current global scenario necessitates worldwide initiatives to manage the impact of natural disasters and advancements.

The devastating implications of nuclear, biological, and chemical (NBC) warfare have been acknowledged by the international community. Accordingly, disasters will continue to be a severe issue for India to overcome soon. On the one hand, a multi-pronged plan for overall disaster management, including prevention, readiness, response, and recovery, is required, while on the other hand, development initiatives must be launched. The natural, environmental, social, economic, health, and engineering sciences are all included in the field of DRR in its broadest sense, and scientific competencies are construed widely to cover all essential scientific and technological tools and expertise (Southgate et al., 2013).The social sciences, in particular, have played a critical role in the creation of new perspectives on risks, vulnerabilities, and widespread poverty as well as people's responsibilities in DRR. The challenge of persuading policymakers to spend significantly on DRR is dependent on social scientists' insights into legislation, economics, and governance and their particular contribution to disaster data gathering and analysis (Basher, 2013).

Keeping in view the increasing new emerging challenges in DRR, the training programme was intended to discuss the strategies for states to cope with the new emerging challenges in DRR. An online training programme on 'Emerging Challenges for Disaster Risk Reduction: New Strategy and 15th Finance Commission' was held from 27 May to 29 May 2021, between 3:00 pm and 5:00 pm. The programme was jointly organised by the Department of Social Work, Central University of Tamil Nadu and the National Institute of Disaster Management, New Delhi.

Aim of Training

The 'Emerging Challenges for Disaster Risk Reduction: New Strategy and 15th Finance Commission' training was intended for officials of health, education, panchayat raj, rural development, revenue, women and child welfare, police department, any other relevant department officials as well as students, faculty, departments at the state level, administrative training institutions, and non-governmental professionals to assist in the development of their knowledge, skills, and perspectives on new emerging challenges in DRR.

Objectives of the Training Programme

At the end of this course, participants would be able to:

1. explain the impacts of disaster on the development
2. identify and list new emerging challenges in DRR
3. explain the process of mainstreaming DRR into the development plan
4. draft and apply strategies for the new emerging challenges in DRR

Inaugural Session

Speaker: Professor Y. Satyanarayana

Founding Vice-Chancellor, Damodaram Sanjivayya National Law University and Former Vice-Chancellor, Andhra Pradesh Law University, Visakhapatnam

Professor Y. Satyanarayana mentioned that in the present situation where the whole world is fighting with the COVID-19 pandemic, it has become the responsibility of all individuals to follow COVID appropriate behaviour. The guidelines published by the Centre for Disease Control and Prevention has included the major community mitigation strategies to limit the spread of COVID-19. It includes social distancing, disease education, community action plans, contact tracing, personal protective measures of wearing a mask, cleaning and disinfection, etc. Therefore, robust regulations along with self-regulation are indeed the need of the hour to minimise and prevent the pandemic rather than blaming the situation.

Session on Do's and Don'ts on COVID-19

Speaker: Balu

Child Centric Disaster Risk Reduction Centre, Centre at National Institute of Disaster Management

Balu, employed at the National Institute of Disaster Management (NIDM) at the Child Centric Disaster Risk Reduction Centre in the southern campus, Andhra Pradesh presented the topic on do's and don'ts of COVID. The COVID-19 pandemic has resulted in the death of millions of people around the world and continues to be a major global hazard (Jordan, Yoeli, and Rand, 2021). It is caused by one virus, called severe acute respiratory syndrome coronavirus 2, or SARS-CoV-2. It affects different people differently however, the commonly found symptoms of COVID-19 are cough, sore throat, fever, tiredness, aches and pains, difficulty in breathing, loss of taste or smell, headache, etc. Most people experience symptoms ranging from mild to moderate. When Dr. Balu visited three districts in Tamil Nadu, he found that COVID has spread to all the villages. He could find that in each village almost hundred to two hundred people were showing symptoms of COVID but they were reluctant to consult a doctor. Most people followed unscientific methods and treatments in curing the disease and completely ignored COVID etiquettes. These are some of the major reasons for the spread of the disease.

Therefore, it remains essential that even after the introduction of vaccines, people must continue to engage in behaviours that help avoid infection such as masking, personal hygiene, and physical distancing (Anderson et al., 2020; Su et al., 2021). Dr Balu emphasised the significance of educating the do's and don'ts of COVID-19 and making others follow them. The major do's are to wash hands often by using sanitiser or soap and water, cover nose and mouth while sneezing and coughing. If a person is not having anything to cover their nose and mouth, they can also use their flexed elbow. In case some tissues are used while sneezing or coughing, they must be disposed of in a closed dustbin.

If a person feels unhealthy, even though they are symptomatic or asymptomatic, it is important to seek a doctor's help. He also highlighted the need to avoid going to large gatherings like marriage, religious rituals, etc. As the threat of coronavirus transmitting from humans to humans is higher, social isolation is the best precautionary measure to be adopted to prevent the spread of the disease. The major don'ts that must be practised are to avoid close contact with people who are experiencing any symptoms of COVID, practising social distancing with people even if they are asymptomatic, avoid touching eyes, nose and mouth. It is very difficult to ensure these practices among but considering the vulnerability, it is important to educate them and help them to learn COVID appropriate behaviour. Spitting in public places is another dangerous behaviour that must be avoided to save lives and to decrease the risk of the spread of COVID-19.

The following precautionary measures were suggested to reduce the risk of coronavirus infection:

- **Washing hands:** The safety of a person is in their hands. Wash hands for at least 20 seconds, till elbow, with soap and water. Alcohol-based hand sanitiser (with at least 60 per cent alcohol) should be used in situations where soap and water facility is not available.
- **Wearing a mask:** Use hand sanitizer or wash your hands before touching the mask for wearing. While putting on a face mask ensure that your nose and mouth are fully covered. Remember to wash your hands or use hand sanitiser while removing the mask. Moreover, it is not advisable to reuse a mask. The clinical masks are to be disposed of after a single use and cloth masks can be washed properly and dried under sunlight before reusing them.
- **Social distancing:** Ensure to maintain at least 1 metre distance in crowded places, switch to the virtual platforms, and keep the number of guests minimal if social events cannot be postponed. Try not to visit crowded or public places as far as possible and avoid non-essential social, commercial, religious, cultural, sporting events, etc. Avoid shaking hands and hugging as a matter of greeting.
- **Home quarantine:** If a person is in home quarantine, they must stay in a well-ventilated single room with an attached toilet facility. The relatives must maintain a distance of at least 1 metre with them. The person in home quarantine must stay away from elderly people, pregnant women, and children. Avoid sharing the household items with the infected person and the person must wear a mask. The surfaces frequently touched by the infected person should be disinfected.
- **Protect children:** Avoid taking children to public places and ensure that someone is taking care of the child. To protect the children from the pandemic, they must follow certain etiquettes. Ensure that they wash their hands frequently, teach them to maintain social distancing,

and encourage indoor games and not shared indoor games. Parents must clean their toys and other things regularly.

Maintaining these acceptable behaviours is very critical considering the bimodal distribution of COVID-19 and the probability of a new wave of COVID-19 appearing soon. Apart from the general public, the responsibility of government and policymakers in supporting and maintaining these appropriate behaviour changes by providing an enabling environment is very important.(Gupta et al., 2021).Individuals with some critical health concerns are always advised to consult a doctor before vaccination. He made a special note that there is no proof for any deaths due to vaccination.

Session on Disaster and Development Resilient Infrastructure and Emerging Challenges for Disaster Risk Reduction

Speaker: Santosh Kumar

Professor and Head, Governance and Inclusive Disaster Risk Reduction Division, National Institute of Disaster Management, Ministry of Home Affairs, Government of India, New Delhi

Professor Santosh Kumar mentioned that disasters affect sectors of housing and human settlements, health, education, agriculture, industry, electricity, communications, and transport. Natural disasters cause considerable economic loss in developing countries and their low-income populations bear the burden of the consequences. The intensity of natural activities has gone very high in the last 20 years. If we look at India's profile, there is no place that is not prone to disasters including drought, heavy rains, earthquakes, urban flooding, tsunami, landslides, etc. We aspire to achieve all sustainable development goals that lead to people's welfare which will start only when there is no poverty. When disasters happen, it affects the most vulnerable populations such as economically deprived communities, women and children, the elderly, people with chronic health conditions as well as remote rural and urban areas with limited access to healthcare and migrants.

Professor Santosh Kumar also shared that disasters always lead to the collapse of education, health, road, communications, and connectivity infrastructure. Only when we protect our schools, hospitals, individual houses, roads, bridges, highways, electricity distribution poles, telephone lines, and other infrastructure that support the development of a community, we can expect the development to happen. If we are aspiring for human development indicators such as good health and quality education, we need to protect the investment that we have made in our infrastructure which will pay dividends for development.

When the tsunami occurred in 2004, the development infrastructure in over seven Indian states was devastated. Hence, we are not resilient and capable enough to protect our infrastructures against disasters. If we look at the series of earthquakes that have happened in the past, cyclones and floods have been happening always. We also hear the news and data that so many people and infrastructure got affected. During the 2018 Kerala floods, every development sector got affected. The volume of loss was 28,000 crore. This amount was invested in the development sector through which sustainable development goals can be achieved. Hence, the state had to rebuild and recreate the whole infrastructure. The rebuilding cost was estimated to be 29,000 crores. So, the total loss of the flooding is about 60,000 crores. If two or three states are affected by a disaster in a year, it would significantly affect the country's development. The protection we make for our infrastructure against any disaster would contribute to the development and people's welfare such that human development indicators, social indicators, economic indicators, and environmental indicators can be fulfilled.

The speaker also mentioned that during disasters, services from health centres and educational institutions are greatly affected as their infrastructure collapses. When we invest in development infrastructure, we have to focus on the design of infrastructure that would withstand any calamity and disaster and continue rendering its services to the community during natural activities. In Gujarat during the 2001 earthquake, the main hospital was devastated and there was no health service available to the people. During recovery in Gujarat, they applied the base isolation technique in hospitals which would prevent collapse against an earthquake.

The cities now in India are overwhelmed by population density. By 2050, 50 per cent of the population will move to urban areas. This is a big challenge for urban planning experts and infrastructure planners to plan for, adjusting to this urban population density. In that scenario, even a small disaster can affect a large population and hence we need to revisit our development strategies in each sector. The role of universities and educational institutions is very important in guiding our planners and policymakers in governance and planning for education, health, road, communication, and other relevant development sectors.

Due to certain disasters that happened in India in the last decade and the COVID pandemic, it will be difficult for India to attain Sustainable Development Goals (SDGs). This will result in increased poverty and more people suffering from hunger, inaccessibility to quality education and health as well as gender inequality. The biggest challenge for policy makers is to analyse the risk in advance and plan and find out opportunities to achieve SDGs, the Sendai Framework, and the Paris agreement on climate change. The policymakers need to focus on risk management, carbon emission, and climate change to accelerate the development of the country.

The speaker also stated that risk reduction should happen at the individual level, community level, district level, state level, and the country as a whole. Individuals' mindsets and attitudes towards risk reduction have to be built to reduce the effects of disasters. If we are the ones who are creating the risks, we can also take the necessary steps to reduce the risks as well. Intergovernmental processes and partnerships are needed to meet emerging challenges for DRR. Knowledge, evidence generation and application are key aspects for building a development resilient infrastructure

Stronger regional cooperation and collaboration is needed to manage disasters and pandemic health emergencies. Pooling of regional resources, technologies and innovations-risk analytics, tele-medicine, tele-education, and remote learning will assist in combating COVID-19. During a disaster, preparedness with DRR tools saves lives and protects people in crisis. Early detection, early warning, rapid diagnostics, risk governance, communication, tele-health, and delivery of services are important components of the DRR process. Multi-stakeholders participation, risk data and information, good practice, policy guidance, tools, and capacity building can support in designing constructive intervention programmes to address the needs of all sections of the community affected by the disaster.

To a question asked by a participant about addressing economic loss due to the pandemic, the speaker responded that the second wave of COVID has hit India severely and a third wave is also anticipated. We need to have a robust kind of economic system to handle the crisis. Lockdowns, partial or complete, have been enforced in different states to protect people's lives. In this year, economic growth might be slower but when it recovers, it will recover fast. The government needs to support the sectors that have been severely affected by the pandemic. The moment we control the pandemic situation, our economy will be bouncing back.

To a question asked by a participant about the efforts that were executed to rebuild tsunami-affected places, the speaker responded that post-disaster recovery was good when the tsunami hit different places in Tamil Nadu. The recovery was supported by the World Bank and Asian development bank. The efforts of the district collectors in tsunami-affected parts were quite remarkable. The state and national government collaboration were also effective in the recovery within a short duration. Teamwork and larger community engagement played a key role in the rebuilding process. The application lessons learnt from Gujarat's earthquake were helpful during recovery from the tsunami.

To a question asked by a participant about protecting economically poor people who live in disaster-prone areas, the speaker responded that living in a city is expensive. To live in a safer place is not affordable to many poor people and hence they prefer to settle down in places such as around river banks or on the seashore. We need to work to reduce poverty. We need strong social security measures to support poor people. Academia and researchers have an important role to bring innovations to suggest governments to bring economically deprived communities out of poverty which would prevent them to settle down in disaster-prone areas and protect their lives.

Session on Strategies to Overcome Emerging Challenges in Disaster Risk Reduction with Special Reference to Children

Speaker: Dr. Balu I.

Child Centric Disaster Risk Reduction Centre, National Institute of Disaster Management, Delhi

Dr Balu mentioned that children are directly affected by any disaster. Karnataka and Andhra Pradesh have experienced ten droughts from 2001 to 2015, which led to 36.2 per cent of stunting and 26.1 per cent of wasting among children in Karnataka. The loss of lives of children has been higher than adults. Disasters separate children from their families and critical infrastructures, which are vital for their survival, also get damaged during a disaster. Disaster risk reduction is best handled when situation analysis for development programme creation takes into account the population's age and gender-related demands. The requirement for care, protection, and the magnitude of children's survival dependency changes from the prenatal stage onwards. During disasters and complicated events, duty bearers' services are generally a chance of being undermined. Following a disaster, social norms/practices such as gender inequality, early marriages, child labour, and so on become more pronounced, affecting children at various stages of their lives. A child's life can be classified into different periods based on their age and risk level. When designing child-centric DRR initiatives, it is essential to address age-specific, gender-specific requirements, and vulnerabilities.

Dr Balu also indicated the life cycle approach for DRR. Prenatal is the first phase of a child's development. The first 1000 days of their life are the most fragile and highly vulnerable. At this point, childhood development necessitates prompt crucial attention and care. Children and their mothers are both extremely vulnerable to a disaster's direct and indirect activities. Emergencies and climate change situations as well as disaster exposure can heighten a child's vulnerabilities. At this stage of their lives, children's needs and rights include timely access to obstetrics care for labour, prenatal care, and postnatal services. It is critical to keep track of pregnant women, assess their progress, and implement specialised tactics to enhance institutional delivery during a disaster. We must also guarantee that resources for menstrual hygiene, soaps, suitable housing, and other Water, sanitation and hygiene (WASH) services are available during a disaster. For the timely restoration of disaster-affected families, multiple social protection measures like public distribution systems are required.

Children in the second phase (0-2 years) must be exclusively breastfed and after 6 months, they can be supplemented with suitable alternative food. Lactation failure, largely as a consequence of emotional shock, is a big concern during and after disasters, as it can have a serious impact on a child's health. An additional factor, that might have a significant effect on a child's growth and survival, is the loss of caring. The immunisation protocol can be disrupted when people are displaced as a result of calamities. The third phase of a child's life (3-5 years) is the most significant time of their life cycle because this is when the majority of their cognitive development occurs. Special care is a vital success factor in a child's growth. Anganwadis can be damaged as a result, causing problems with nutrition and early childhood schooling. Formal education, sports, and activities are all important parts of a child's development throughout the fourth period (6 to 12 years, middle childhood), according to the speaker. When a disaster strikes, all of these things are affected and interrupted. After a crisis, school days will be lost since schools will most likely be used as shelters for displaced people. Supporting children's education allows parents to concentrate on recovery and rebuilding needs rather than worrying about their children's security and safety. Emphasis on sexual and reproductive health is critical in the fifth period (12-18 years, adolescence). Disasters have an impact on menstrual hygiene as well. Moreover, adolescence might begin to take on the role of active change agents. Adolescent participation in DRR activities can aid their active participation and safety. Adolescents can prepare for adulthood by maintaining their learning opportunities, improving their hygiene, participating in sports, and participating in recreational activity through the post-disaster early restoration process.

To a question asked by a participant about the psychological effects of a disaster on children, the speaker responded that children are very much stressed and they experience psychological trauma when a disaster happens. Parents need to be aware of how to educate their children to cope with disasters. The effect of trauma on a child's mind persists for a longer duration. The children who experienced a tsunami and lost their loved ones still carry painful memories. Though they have become adults now, the psychological impact continues. There is a need for psychological counselling and a support system for children to cope with the trauma they experience during a disaster.

To a question asked by a participant about managing stress among school children when they do not have much opportunity to meet their friends or attend classroom discussions during the pandemic situation, the speaker replied that children were not able to meet their friends and hence they needed to be supported by connecting to their friends over the phone. Education through the online mode is not reaching many students as they are not interested in learning online. Only when they realise that education is important, will they show interest in their classes. Parents must spend their time with children and discuss with them their education and interests. They must be encouraged to play indoor games and play with siblings so that they can feel relaxed.

To a question asked by a participant about protecting children against child abuse, the speaker responded that first children should not be left alone. It is important to ensure that children are always monitored by someone so that abuse can be avoided. Second, they should be educated against abuse. Third, except mother and father, others should not be allowed to touch children. At least these three things should be followed to avoid abuse. If one is to witness a child marriage, they must inform the nearest police station or village administrative officer and take necessary actions or convince the parents to not agree to child marriages.

Interactive session on Disaster Funding Regarding 15th Finance Commission, Public Policy for Disaster Risk Reduction and Disaster Development Resilient Infrastructure

Speaker: Professor Santosh Kumar, PhD

Professor and Head, Governance and Inclusive Disaster Risk Reduction Division, National Institute of Disaster Management, Ministry of Home Affairs, Government of India, New Delhi

PARTICIPANT: How can we enhance the responsibilities of the government, community and individuals in DRR, with special reference to the current pandemic's context?

SPEAKER: Each disaster is unique demanding unique response patterns and the first principle of DRR is to be adaptive to any disaster in planning the responses. The intensity and size of the disaster, along with system capacity and local community engagement, determine the disaster response strategies.

In our system, one ministry serves as the nodal ministry for a particular type of disaster while other ministries complement the response in various capacities. For example, the Ministry of Health and Family Welfare is the nodal ministry at the central level for biological disasters like pandemics and at the state level the Principal Secretary for Health takes the lead role. Disaster response is a state subject in India and mostly the state principal secretary for the respective department leads the response. However, in developing countries like India, disaster response is still a grey area.

In the case of COVID-19, the size and intensity of the disaster is huge than estimated in the risk assessment as well as exhaustive to the resources and health systems, resulting in a supply and demand deficiency. Resource allocations are done based on the risk assessment process which informs on the size and intensity of a disaster. If the size is underestimated, it will exhaust the resources and the systems.

Even if the risk assessment gages the size of a disaster precisely, if the size and intensity is huge to the capacity of systems and resources, it can still be exhaustive. The pandemic follows a non-predictable trend in intensity and hence planning effective response strategies is challenging. All the stakeholders including the nodal ministry, other authorities, the local community, and the public were overwhelmed in the response process.

It was also observed that between waves 1 and 2, our cautionary approaches were relaxed as the True Positive Rate (TPR) showed a downward trend. We eased restrictions in public gatherings, attempted normalcy in life assuming the downward trend as an end of the pandemic, often neglecting the COVID appropriate behaviours. In addition, vaccines were not invented during that particular period, which was an add-on risk. Usually, when the systems are exhausted and overwhelmed, the local communities tend to evolve with self-management systems supporting the affected people. Many Western countries faced a public health system exhaustion during the first wave (for example Italy, Germany, and the US), but they used their experiences as precautions during the second wave. However, India could not do the same with our poor institutional learning memories. All these cumulatively resulted in a high intensive second wave with a failed system.

Unfortunately, we are following a similar trend in the third wave as well. As the TRP goes down, we tend to relax the social distancing norms and attempt to normalise our daily activities and the community response systems wind up. The public health system should inform the local government and the public on the intensity and size of the disaster and should work in collaboration with other stakeholders.

PARTICIPANT: Migration and disaster management: There is a perspective that population movements provide useful elements towards DRR. How do the underlying factors like labour migration lead to a risk enhancement in a disaster situation like a pandemic? How does population movements contribute towards DRR?

SPEAKER: Labour migration is common in drought-prone areas and experiences underlying challenges. It follows different trends like in some cases, only the male members of the family migrate for work and in some other cases, the entire family migrates. When the poor from the drought-hit regions migrate for work, they end up in the city outskirts or slum locations that lack the basic amenities and infrastructure facilities. If they move as a family, women and children suffer due to the poor living conditions. The safety of girls and women is also at stake as the settlements, as well as the work locations, do not have proper sanitation facilities (availability of toilets, water supply, housing, etc.). If only the male members migrate, the women and children are forced to work to support the family's daily expenses.

Poverty induced migrations and reverse migrations: Locations with high-frequency disasters like floods, drought, etc., fail to generate sustainable livelihoods for their population which induces migration. This poverty-induced labour migration has happened pre-pandemic as well as during the pandemic. We have witnessed reverse migrations as well where the migrant labourers returned to their original location as the lockdowns restricted their workdays with limited access to support services such as food and healthcare, market closure, etc. This has stressed the disaster response strategies of the district administration, both at the urban as well as the rural locations, where they originally belong to.

The duration of a disaster is another determining factor that controls the extent of population movements. For example, cyclones have high intensity but are shorter and it is observed that relocated people return to their native places soon after the cyclonic days and normalcy is resumed. However, flood-prone areas face waterlogging and infrastructure destruction which require a long term recovery and reconstruction process. Hence, a long term migration is anticipated. Population movements influence risk enhancement depending on the nature of the disaster and underlying factors for migration.

PARTICIPANT: How can we improve India's performance on SDGs as a strategy towards improving the DRR, especially in the present context where we have consistent poor performance for the last 5 years (113-117 among 165 countries)?

SPEAKER: India has faced various disasters including the pandemic that diverted its investment on SDG indicators. India has faced challenges that restricted its investment in SDG indicators. Pandemic has been prevalent for at least two years. Moreover, our states perform unevenly on the SDG as well as the Millennium Development Goals, with outliers on both sides. Progress on the sustainable development goals depends on how the National Institution for Transforming India

(NITI AYOG) coordinates with the states. Disasters and pandemics have negatively affected the progress but we need to work side-by-side on the SDGs along with the disaster response, which would be challenging in the current context though.

PARTICIPANT: Some disasters are annual and finite. However, the current pandemic COVID-19 had a sudden onset and is infinite. How has the finance commission approached this disaster?

SPEAKER: Disaster funding is required in three stages: pre-disaster management, managing rescue and rehabilitation during the disaster, and addressing long term impacts. Until the 15th commission, there was no specific approach towards pre-disaster and long term impacts mitigation. States were not supported for response and relief. National Disaster Management Act (2005) suggests pre-disaster mitigation fund for reducing the risk factors at state and local levels. Earlier each sector/ department should have a proportion of its development fund allocated for DRR in the respective sector. However, with the 15th finance commission, a separate fund is allocated for DRR. There are provisions for requesting additional funds if it is found insufficient.

PARTICIPANT: Can you comment on the interlink between disaster management and the development of a nation?

SPEAKER: Keeping the infrastructure disaster-resilient can reduce the expenses on disaster management at the cost of development initiatives. Each development project should include DRR and management plans converging different aspects like development, DRR through resilient infrastructure, and environment protection.

PARTICIPANT: How does our scientific expertise and technology support reducing disaster risk? During disasters, governments cut the expenditure on other sectors for mobilising money for disaster response. How does it affect economic development?

SPEAKER: During disasters, states face a huge loss in infrastructure that challenges their economic development. In such cases, states will try to mobilise money from different sources- state and local governments, diverting funds from other departments, grant funding, and loans for infrastructure reconstruction. Diverting development funds may sound unethical but some things need to be done with prioritisation.

PARTICIPANT: How can we prepare our children to face pandemics in future?

SPEAKER: We need to introduce DRR and disaster management components in the curriculum using a multi-disciplinary approach. Young students can be trained in disaster risks and recovery as well as in mitigating geographic area specific disaster risks. These precautionary measures can reduce the impact of a disaster and can enhance recovery. We need to include the national institutions in this process as well.

PARTICIPANT: During health emergencies and pandemics, governments attempt to reduce the doctor-patient ratio which results in increased expenditure in the health sector. How can we look for increasing the number of doctors and health professionals in the country by increasing the number of medical colleges in the country? How can a socialist approach in the health sector be implemented in countries like India?

SPEAKER: Public health investments in India are concentrated in the private sector (70 per cent) and only 30 per cent is handled by the public sector. However, the national disaster management act (2005) allows a state to acquire any private institution for disaster management purposes including healthcare facilities. Since it involves a cost for the government so India needs to expand the scope of its policies to strengthen the public sector investments in healthcare, which is a necessity when high-intensity third wave is anticipated.

PARTICIPANT: What are the DRR plans and disaster management tips for Jammu and Kashmir?

SPEAKER: From the past disaster experiences in Jammu and Kashmir, it requires better landscape development projects to overcome the geographical barriers in rescue operations and recovery. It requires urban planning strategies as well as local community capacity building towards disaster management.

PARTICIPANT: What are precautions that need to be taken towards the third wave of COVID-19?

SPEAKER: Scientists and doctors predict children will be affected more during the third wave however, they have not specified the reasons for the same. It could be because of the non-availability of vaccines for the under 18 population. As a precautionary method, we need to adopt COVID-19 appropriate strategies towards education and should strictly restrain from social gatherings, disciplining ourselves. State-level action plans need to be in place for planning and executing DRR plans for the third wave as well.

PARTICIPANT: Can river interlinking projects address food insecurity with special reference to the northern states?

SPEAKER: Yes, to a certain extent. For example, Telangana has a good system of water management and hence can address the issues of drought. Scientists and the central water commission has many research studies on such models and the possibilities for replicating the same in other locations. However, interlinking rivers is a tremendous and costly task and there are fewer evidence of long-term consequences. More regional research are suggested before we proceed with it.

PARTICIPANT: What is your opinion on a shift towards less water-intensive crops for improved food security, especially in disaster-prone areas?

SPEAKER: Yes, this would be a good strategy in addressing migration. A less water-intensive crop strategy would be a better solution for irrigation issues in drought-prone areas. We need to study more on alternatives like moisture determination (getting water from moisture) and more research on developing crops that require less water but provide more yield. There should be attempts to support farmers in adopting the shifting pattern in cultivation. There should also be a public policy response in this area and their implementation at the local level converse towards disaster management.

Recommendations

1. It is high time for institutions, organisations, and people to develop the quality of resilience to overcome the pandemic situation.
2. In the phase of new emerging challenges in DRR, it is very important to look at the possible role of universities through a joint collaborative effort in DRR.
3. We must make use of the possible utilisation of the available resources for DRR.
4. The state has an important role to provide disaster relief. Robust regulation is required to reduce disasters and each person must carry out their basic responsibilities, particularly in the case of the environment. Everyone has to work together to minimise and prevent calamity rather than blaming each other for the pandemic situation.
5. Intergovernmental processes and partnerships are needed to meet emerging challenges for DRR.

6. Knowledge, evidence generation, and application are key aspects for building development resilient infrastructure.
7. Multi-stakeholders' participation, risk data and information, good practice, policy guidance, tools, and capacity building can support in designing constructive intervention programmes to address the needs of all sections of the community affected by a disaster.
8. Disaster risk can be best addressed if situation analysis for development programme formulation considers age and gender-related needs.
9. There is a need to consider age-specific, gender-specific needs, vulnerabilities, and capacities while designing child-centric DRR activities are designed to execute relevant rehabilitation programmes.
10. Continuity of learning opportunities, hygiene improvement practices, sports, recreation through post-disaster early recovery programmes can enable adolescents to prepare themselves for their transition to adulthood.
11. Various social protection schemes such as the public distribution system are very relevant actions for the early recovery of disaster-impacted families.
12. There is still a long way to go in terms of implementing policies for DRR in all areas of life, as the 15th finance commission has for the first time set out certain priorities and given guidelines on how the funds for disasters can be used effectively by forcing the state to spend on it.

Conclusion

The growing gap between human needs and grab has a direct influence on nature's equilibrium, making a human presence on Earth problematic. Constant calamities affect all aspects of human life including advancement in the human development index. Disasters have also shown the importance of public policy decisions. Delayed policy responses can result in irreversible disruptions. There is a need for diplomatic policies on DRR in all areas. The finance commission has, for the first time, introduced guidelines and set priorities for DRR techniques with a force on the state governments to spend on them.

References

[1] Aitsi-Selmi, A., Murray, V., Wannous, C., Dickinson, C., Johnston, D., Kawasaki, A., & Yeung, T. (2016). 'Reflections on a science and technology

agenda for 21st century disaster risk reduction'. *International Journal of Disaster Risk Science*, 7(1), 1–29.

[2] Anderson, R.M., Heesterbeek, H., Klinkenberg, D., & Hollingsworth, T.D. (2020). 'How will country-based mitigation measures influence the course of the COVID-19 epidemic?' *The Lancet*, 395(10228), 931–934.

[3] Basher, R. (2013). 'Science and Technology for Disaster Risk Reduction: A review of application and coordination needs'. UNISDR Report.

[4] Dekens, J. (2007). 'Local knowledge for disaster preparedness: A literature review'. *International Centre for Integrated Mountain Development (ICIMOD)*.

[5] Gupta, M.K., Bhardwaj, P., Goel, A., Saurabh, S., & Misra, S. (2021). 'COVID-19 appropriate behavior in India: Time to invest for the benefits in future'. *Journal of Family Medicine and Primary Care*, 10(5), 1818.

[6] Izumi, T., Shaw, R., Djalante, R., Ishiwatari, M., & Komino, T. (2019). 'Disaster risk reduction and innovations'. *Progress in Disaster Science*, 2, 100033.

[7] Jordan, J.J., Yoeli, E., & Rand, D.G. (2021). 'Don't get it or don't spread it: Comparing self-interested versus prosocial motivations for COVID-19 prevention behaviors'. *Scientific reports*, 11(1), 1-17. Retrieved from https://doi.org/10.1038/s41598-021-97617-5, accessed on 12 December 2021.

[8] Kadri, A.M. (2019). IAPSM's Textbook of Community Medicine. Jaypee Brothers Medical Publishers.

[9] Kirch, W. (Ed.) (2008). Encyclopedia of Public Health, Volume 1: A-H Volume 2: I-Z. Springer Science & Business Media.

[10] Sanderson, D., & Sharma, A. (2016). 'World disasters report, resilience: Saving lives today, investing for tomorrow'. *International Federation of Red Cross and Red Crescent Societies*.

[11] Southgate, R.J., Roth, C., Schneider, J., Shi, P., Onishi, T., Wenger, D., & Murray, V. Using Science for Disaster Risk Reduction. Report of the UNISDR Scientific and Technical Advisory Committee. UNISDR 2013.

[12] Su, Z., Wen, J., McDonnell, D., Goh, E., Li, X., Šegalo, S., & Xiang, Y.T. (2021). 'Vaccines are not yet a silver bullet: The imperative of continued communication about the importance of COVID-19 safety measures'. *Brain, behavior, & immunity-health*, 12, 100204.

The Editors

Sigamani Panneer, FRSA (Lon), FRSPH (Lon), Raman Fellow (Hosted at UMN, USA) is the Professor and Head of the Department of Social Work, School of Social Sciences and Humanities, Central University of Tamil Nadu, India. A recipient of the prestigious Raman fellowship, he served as Visiting Professor at the School of Public Health, University of Minnesota, USA Tianjin University of Finance and Economics, China, andJishou University, China. He has Master's Degrees in Public Administration and Social Work from the University of Madras, Post Graduate Diploma in Business Administration from Pondicherry University (A Central University), M.Phil and PhD in Public Health from Centre of Social Medicine and Community Health, Jawaharlal Nehru University, New Delhi and Postdoctoral research training (PDF) in Public Health at Division of Environmental Health Sciences, School of Public Health, University of Minnesota (Twin Cities Campus), MN, USA. He has researched various areas relating to new public health management, drug delivery systems, public-private partnerships in healthcare, occupational health and women's health. He has authored articles of national and international repute published by (1) Palgrave Macmillan, (2) Macmillan Publishers Ltd, (3) Sage, (4) Springer, (5) Wiley, (6) Elsevier, (7) Taylor and Francis (8) BMC Tobacco Induced Diseases, (9) Bloomsbury, (10) Economic and Political Weekly, (11) Cambridge Scholars, and (12) Science, etc.

Santhosh Kumar is a disaster risk reduction, policy planning, and capacity development expert with 25 years of experience in different positions in the development planning and disaster risk reduction sector. With a PhD. in Economics, he studied gender and development in the Institute of Development Studies, Sussex, The United Kingdom, and received professional training in disaster risk management from Israel, backed with international work exposure at The World Bank and the Inter-governmental body of South Asian Association for Regional Cooperation. He has an experienced hand in designing, planning, and implementing mitigation and long-term disaster recovery plan and projects. He specialises in disaster management planning, post-disaster loss and needs assessment, recovery, and inclusive disaster risk reduction. At the international level, he has been contributing to shifting international and national policies by engaging himself in dialogues, negotiations, and participating in international strategic conferences.

Balu I is working in Child Centric Disaster Risk Reduction Centre at the National Institute of Disaster Management, Ministry of Home Affairs, Government of India. Previously he served as an Assistant Professor at Rajiv Gandhi National Institute of Youth Development. He has ten years of experience in the development sector. He has received his PhD in Sociology from Madurai Kamaraj University. He has coordinated national-level workshops and training programmes related to youth development and disaster management. He has published two books and more than 25 papers in national and international journals.

Vigneshwaran Subbiah Akkayasamy is a Junior Research Fellow, University Grants Commission-National Eligibility Test, pursuing PhD at the Department of Social Work, School of Humanities and Social Sciences, Central University of Tamil Nadu, Thiruvarur, India. He has completed his M.A. in Social Work and B.Sc. Zoology from The American College (affiliated to Madurai Kamaraj University), Tamil Nadu. His areas of interest include road traffic injuries and mental health. He has worked as a senior community mental health social worker wherein he was part of a multidisciplinary mental health team who worked with the rural communities of Madurai district, Tamil Nadu.

Contributors

Ankathi Raghu is an Associate Professor in the Department of Tourism and Hospitality Management, Central University of Tamil Nadu. He joined the institution in 2019. He started his carrier as a District Tourism Officer and due to his interest in the field of travel and tourism, he has travelled the length and breadth of the country. Later with his interest in academics, he started his journey as an Assistant professor in the tourism and travel sector. So far he has guided research scholars from various universities across the country and has published more than 35 articles in prestigious journals of the sector.

Aswathi K.R. is a Junior Research Fellow in the Department of Social Work, Central University of Tamil Nadu, Thiruvarur, India. She has a Master's degree in Social Work specialising inmedical and psychiatric field from SreeSankaracharya University, Kalady, Kerala. She worked as an Assistant Professor at Anugraha Institute of Social Sciences, Dindigul, Tamil Nadu. During her period of working, she collaborated and supported colleagues and students in research interests and co-curricular activities. Her academic project during post-graduation was on 'Social media in disaster management: An assessment based on Kerala flood 2018'. Her research interest is in the field of disaster risk reduction. Currently, she is working on research related to 'Multistakeholder participation in disaster recovery, a case of post-cyclone Ockhi in the maritime community of Kerala'.

Balu I. is working in CCDRR Centre at the National Institute of Disaster Management, Ministry of Home Affairs, Government of India. Previously, he served as an Assistant Professor at Rajiv Gandhi National Institute of Youth Development. He has two years of research experience from the National Institute of Rural Development and Panchayat Raj (NIRD and PR). Overall, he has thirteen years of experience in disaster and development. He has received his PhD in Sociology from Madurai Kamaraj University. He has coordinated national-level workshops and training programmes, has published two books and more than forty papers in national and international journals.

Hilaria Soundari M. is an Assistant Professor in the Department of Applied Research, Gandhigram Rural Institute, Deemed University, Gandhigram, India. She belongs to the congregation of the sisters of the cross of Chavanod. She is specialised in the fields of development research, gender issues and social work. She received postdoctoral fellowship (2012–14) from UGC, New Delhi. She is working with marginalised women and children for 21 years in rural India and researching their empowerment and sustainable development. She has authored several articles in renowned journals and edited four books.

Josiah Stanely Rose G. is a PhD research scholar in the Department of Social Work, Central University of Tamil Nadu, Thiruvarur, India. He has a Master's in Social Work specialising in the medical and psychiatric field from Bishop Heber College, Tiruchirappalli. He went on to join the Mary Varghese Rehabilitation Institute at Christian Medical College, Vellore as a Medical Social Worker. His work there involved socio-vocational and economic analysis, management of vocational rehabilitation programmes, follow-up of rehabilitated patients, and facilitating community-based rehabilitation initiatives. Josiah firmly believes that any form of rehabilitation should result in community participation. Currently, he is working on research related to psychosocial well-being, employment resettlement, community re-integration, and follow-up strategies among rehabilitated persons with spinal cord injury.

Lekha Bhat is an Assistant Professor at the Department of Epidemiology and Public Health, Central University of Tamil Nadu, India. She has basic training in Public Health with an MPhil and a PhD in Social Medicine and Community Health from Jawaharlal Nehru University (JNU) New Delhi. She has published papers with reputed journals in Springer, Wiley, and Bloomsbury.

Lovelina Little Flower F.X. is a Professor and Head of the Department of Social Work, currently Dean in-charge of College Development Council, Bharathiar University. She pursued her PhD in Social Work from Bharathidasan University and has teaching experience of 26 years. She has produced about eleven PhDs, eleven M.Phil candidates and coordinated projects from University Grants Commission, National Institute of Social Defense, Rashtriya Uchchatar Shiksha Abhiyan, etc.

She has several publications innational and international journals. She has also held positions like Presiding Officer for Internal Compliance Committee, coordinator for Swachh Bharat Mission and Unnat Bharat Abhiyan, Director in-charge for Centre for Collaboration of Industry and Dean for the College Development Council of Bharathiar University.

Mhadeno Y. Humtsoe is a PhD Research Scholar at the Centre for Applied Research, Gandhigram Rural Institute, Gandhigram, Tamilnadu, India. Being a recipient of the National Fellowship for Higher Education of ST Students (NFST), she is pursuing her doctoral studies in the field of livelihood and material healthcare among tribal women. She has served as a faculty member at the University of Science and Technology, Meghalaya. She has also authored research articles in national and international Journals.

Michelle Elizabeth Mathew is a Senior Research Fellow (UGC-NET) at the Department of Social Work, Bharathiar University, Coimbatore. Her research focuses on family and marital relationships in general and marital intimacy and satisfaction in particular. She completed her Master of Social Work from Bharathiar University and also holds an MBA in Human Resource Management from the University of Wales, UK.

Nirmal Kumar K. is pursuing his PhD in Economics at Muthurangam Government Arts College (Autonomous) Vellore, Tamil Nadu. He has written a good number of research articles published in various journals and has edited books. He has also presented papers in many national and international level conferences. He is a member of the Association of Economists of Tamil Nadu (AET).

Premkumar A. is presently a PhD research scholar at the Department of Economics, Sacred Heart College (Autonomous), Tirupattur, Tamil Nadu. He has worked in various research projects funded by international and national agencies such as Gesellschaft fur Internationale Zusammenarbeit (GIZ), Technology Information, Forecasting, and Assessment Council (TIFAC), Ministry of Environment, Forest and Climate Change (MoEFCC), Indian Council of Social Science Research (ICSSR) and Tamil Nadu State Council for Higher Education (TANSHCE). He has written and published several articles in UGC care listed journals and chapters in an edited book published by Springer Nature. He is also a recipient of the National Fellowship for Higher Education of ST Students (NFST) by the Ministry of Tribal Affairs (Government of India) for his PhD.

Raja P. is currently working as an Assistant Professor in the Department of Tourism and Hospitality Management, the Central University of Tamil Nadu. He joined the institution in the year 2019. He has extensive knowledge and more than ten years of experience in the field of hospitality industry. Due to his interest in research in the field of the hospitality sector, he has published research journals in Elsevier and UGC care list journals.

Renaldo S. Rajkumar has completed his under-graduation degree in Psychology, post-graduation degree in Social Work specialising in Human Resource Management, and is currently pursuing his PhD in Community Development specific to elderly care management from Bharathiar University. He has undertaken research studies for a private organisation. He serves as an advisory committee member for Santhom Social Service Society (Coimbatore) and Brothers Integrated Rural Development Society(Bengaluru). He has also been invited as a resource person for research and skill development forums. He has participated in training programmes, seminars,and workshops and has presented research papers at conferences.

Robert Ramesh Babu P. is a Research Scholar in the Department of Social Work, Central University of Tamil Nadu, Thiruvarur. He was the former Vice-Principal and Head of the Department of Social Work, Don Bosco College, Dharmapuri. He has a wide experience in teaching, administration and organising extension activities. He did his post-graduate studies at Loyola College, Chennai and M.Phil in Bishop Heber College, Tiruchirapalli. He is currently working on the concept of happiness at workplace for his doctoral studies.

Salaijayamani A. is a PhD research scholar in the Department of Economics, Sacred Heart College (Autonomous), Tirupattur, Tamil Nadu. His research interest is in agricultural economics concerning agricultural marketing, minimum support price, and Agricultural Produce Market Committee (APMC). He has presented many papers in national and international conferences and also published two papers in reputed journals. He is also worked as a field investigator for agencies like the Indian Council of Social Science Research (ICSSR) and the All India Society for Development (AISD), New Delhi.

Santosh J.S. is a Senior Research Fellow (UGC-NET) working in the Department of Social Work, Bharathiar University, Coimbatore. He was awarded Junior Research Fellowship (JRF) by UGC- New Delhi, to pursue a doctoral degree in Social Work. Before joining the department, he worked with health resource groups in Tamil Nadu in thrust areas like community action for health, social determinants of health, health system accountability, school mental health, and literacy.

Shahin Sultana A. is a Professor in the Department of Social Work, School of Social Sciences and International Studies, Pondicherry University. She has specialised in medical and psychiatric social work and her thrust areas of research and training include youth, children, women and families. She teaches psychology for social work practice, social policy and social welfare administration, medical social work, and public health for social workers.

Sigamani Panneer is a Professor and Head, the Department of Social Work, School of Social Sciences and Humanities, Central University of Tamil Nadu, India. A recipient of the prestigious Raman fellowship, he served as visiting Professor at the School of Public Health, University of Minnesota(USA), Tianjin University of Finance and Economics(China), and Jishou University(China). He has authored articles of national and international repute published by Palgrave Macmillan, Sage, Springer, Wiley, Elsevier, BMC, EPW and Bloomsbury.

Sivakami V. is a Guest Faculty in the Department of Tourism and Hospitality Management, the Central University of Tamil Nadu, joined the institution in the year 2021. She started her carrier as an industry professional and shifted to academics with a passion to teach in the tourism and travel sector. With more than five years of teaching experience, she also completed her research degree with a specialisation in the field of sustainable tourismand published articles in journals like Elsevier, Scopus, and UGC care listed journals.

Sivasankar V. is presently working as an Assistant Professor at the Post-Graduate and Research Department of Economics, Muthurangam Government Arts College (Autonomous) Vellore, Tamil Nadu. He did his PhD at the Centre for Economic Studies and Planning (CESP), Jawaharlal Nehru University, New Delhi. He has completed three major projects funded by Indian Council of Social Science Research (ICSSR) and UGC. His area of interest includes development economics with a focus on agrarian relations, urban labour market, labour market discrimination, and gender relation.

Sulochana Shekhar is the Dean of the School of Earth Sciences and Head of the Department of Geography at the Central University of Tamil Nadu, Thiruvarur, India. She is the proud recipient of the Erasmus Mundus (European Commission) Fellowship, Commonwealth Academic Fellowship (United Kingdom) and Endeavor Research Fellowship (Australia). Her research interests include urban geography, the application of remote sensing and geospatial techniques in urban environments. She is presently teaching urban geography and the fundamentals and applications of geoinformatics at the post-graduation level. She has worked on cellular automata-based urban growth models and urban sprawl assessment using entropy for her doctoral research. Object-based image analysis was the main theme of her post-doctoral research. She has previously worked on projects involving spatial decision support systems for slums and extraction of slums and urban green space using object-based image analysis.

Sunitha V.G. is a research scholar with the Department of Social Work, Central University of Tamil Nadu. She has completed her Master's in Social work from Mahatma Gandhi University, Kerala. She associated with Marian College, Kuttikkana for a short duration as a coordinator for the community college programme. In her current capacity, she is associated with the Programme Quality Department of World Vision India, a child-focused community development organisation and is based in Chennai. Currently, she handles programme evaluations. She has been associated with the World Vision for the last 10 years and has worked with urban programming and research-based in Bhopal and Delhi under various roles before moving to programme evaluations in 2017. Her research interests include urban housing, relocations, urban social stratifications, and development challenges.

Tresa Sugirtha J. is an Assistant Professor, the Department of Social Work, P.S.G College of Arts and Science, Coimbatore. She has secured first ranks at the university level in Bachelor of Social Work (BSW) and Master of Social Work (MSW). Her areas of interest include children, youth, families, climate change and mental health. At present, she is undertaking a research project on the 'Psycho-social impact of intermittent partner absence among merchant seafarers and their spouses' funded by UGC, New Delhi.

Udhayakumar P. is an Assistant Professor in the Department of Social Work, School of Social Sciences, Central University of Tamil Nadu, India. He has a Bachelor's degree in Physics, a Master's Degree in Social Work from Urumu Dhanalakshmi College and PhD in Social Work from Bharathidasan University. He is passionate about working and researching in the field of mental health. He has extensively contributed to the literature of social work practice in mental health through his publication, convening programmes and establishing research networks. His other research interests are in the field of gerontological social work, strengths-based social work, spirituality, and health. He has worked with many non-government organisation (NGO) as a social worker. He values his prolonged engagement with counselling services, particularly as a student counsellor, National Service Scheme Programme Officer and most recently, as a member of District Level Inspection Committee of District Child Protection Unit, Thiruvarur.

Vigneshwaran Subbiah Akkayasamy is pursuing his PhD with a Junior Research Fellowship funded by the UGC in the Department of Social Work, School of Humanities and Social Sciences, the Central University of Tamil Nadu (by an Act of Parliament) Thiruvarur, India. He completed his M.A. Social Work in 2009 and B.Sc. Zoology in 2006 from The American College (affiliated to Madurai Kamaraj University), Tamilnadu. He worked as a senior community mental health social worker as part of a multidisciplinary mental health team at Shant Manas, an NGO dedicated to the service of rural people suffering from mental health difficulties and associated conditions, operating near Madurai(Tamilnadu) for nine years (2009–2018). He is also a life member of the Indian Society of Professional Social Work (ISPSW). His research interests include mental health and road traffic injuries.

Xavier Susairaj A. is Associate Professor and Head of the Department of Economics, Sacred Heart College (Autonomous), Tirupattur. He is a visiting fellow at the Centre for the Crop Science division of Biological Resources and Science, Chonbuk National University, South Korea and a Fulbright visiting scholar in 2010 at Florida International University at Miami, Florida State, USA. He has been awarded the young economist award by the association of economists of Tamil Nadu in 2010. He has written three books and has authored numerous articles. He has completed four major and minor research projects for University Grants Commission and Indian Council of Social Science Research. He has participated in many national and international conferences and presented papers in Japan, Jeiju island, South Korea, Singapore, Thailand and chaired the sessions. He has guided seventeen M.Phil, fourPhD scholars and currently guiding two PhD scholars.